Sheltered English/ESL Manual

GRADE ONE

SENIOR AUTHOR

Stephen D. Krashen

HARCOURT BRACE & COMPANY

Orlando Atlanta Austin Boston San Francisco Chicago Dallas New York
Toronto London

ISBN 0-15-307434-5

3 4 5 6 7 8 9 10 082 99 98 97

Contents

Harcourt Brace School Publishers

About the Author

"Free voluntary reading is the most powerful tool we have in language education."

Dr. Stephen D. Krashen is a professor of Education at the University of Southern California. He is the author of more than 160 articles and books in the fields of neurolinguistics, second-language acquisition, literacy, and bilingual education. He has made significant contributions to these fields and is a prominent educator and a compelling speaker.

In 1982 Dr. Krashen was the winner of the Mildenberger Award, which was presented to honor his book *Second Language Acquisition and Second Language Learning* (Prentice Hall). In 1985 he was the co-winner of the Pimsleur Award given by the American Council of Foreign Language Teachers for the best published article. Dr. Krashen's most recent books are *Fundamentals of Language Education* (Laredo Publishing Co.) and *The Power of Reading* (Libraries Unlimited).

His own personal history of reading comic books as a child supports his idea that "free voluntary reading is the most powerful tool we have in language education."

A man of many interests, Steve Krashen holds a black belt in Tae Kwon Do and was the winner of the 1978 Venice Beach Open Incline Press Championship.

Harcourt Brace School Publishers

ENGLISH LANGUAGE ACQUISITION

The principles underlying successful programs for limited-English-proficient students are the same principles underlying successful foreign language programs and language arts programs for first language and literacy development. The following are a few fundamental hypotheses.

Acquisition-Learning Hypothesis

This hypothesis claims that we have two ways of developing ability in language. *Language acquisition* is a subconscious process; that is, while it is happening we do not know it is happening. In addition, once an aspect of language is acquired, we are not usually aware of it. The knowledge is stored subconsciously in our brains. "Picking up a language" is another way to say "language acquisition."

Language learning is what we did in school. It is a conscious process; when we are learning, we know we are learning. Also, learned knowledge is represented consciously in the brain. In non-technical language, when we talk about "rules" and "grammar," we are usually talking about language learning.

Error correction helps learning. When we make a mistake and someone corrects it, we are supposed to change our conscious version of the rule. If a limited-English-proficient student says, "I comes to school every day," and the teacher says, "No, it's 'I come to school,'" the student is supposed to realize that the *-s* doesn't belong on the first-person singular verb but on the third-person singular verb. This scenario may seem reasonable to the grammarian, but as most readers know, correction does not have this effect. As we shall see, error correction and conscious learning are very limited.

Natural Order Hypothesis

This hypothesis claims that we acquire (not learn) grammatical rules of language in a predictable order. Some aspects of grammar tend to be acquired early, while others are acquired late. In English, for example, the *-ing* marker (John is swimming) tends to be acquired early. However, the *-s* marker (He goes to work every day) tends to be acquired much later. In English, as in the first language, there may be six months to a year between acquisition of these two grammatical markers, and in English as a second language among adults the third-person singular verb form may never be acquired. We all know people who speak English as a second language very well but who have not acquired the third-person singular *-s*.

The natural order does not proceed from simple to complex. Some structures that look easy to linguists are acquired late, while others that are very hard to describe are acquired early. What is significant is that the natural order cannot be changed. It is immune to deliberate teaching. We can drill the third-person singular verb form for weeks, but it will not be acquired "until its time has come."

He go to work every day.

He goes to work every day.

Monitor Hypothesis

This hypothesis attempts to explain how acquisition and learning are used. Language is normally produced using our acquired linguistic competence. Consciously learned knowledge (knowledge "about language") has only one function—as a Monitor or editor.

To clarify the role of conscious learning, we can describe what happens in foreign language use. Suppose you are trying to speak your intermediate Spanish or French or German. The sentence you are about to speak pops into your mind. Then, just before you actually say it, you scan the sentence internally to think about the rules you learned in school. You make corrections using these rules. This illustrates the use of the Monitor.

The Monitor can make a small contribution to accuracy, but it is very limited. To use the Monitor, we must know the rules, think about the rules, and have time to apply the rules. Even for adults with extensive knowledge of grammar, these conditions are met only when they take grammar tests and when they edit their writing. Even then, the Monitor makes a very modest contribution to accuracy. For children, conscious knowledge of grammar plays hardly any role.

Input Hypothesis

This is the central hypothesis in current language acquisition theory. It claims that we acquire language in only one way—when we understand what people tell us and when we understand what we read. We acquire language, in other words, when we obtain *comprehensible input.*

The Input Hypothesis can be restated in terms of the Natural Order Hypothesis, that we acquire the rules of language in a simple, linear order—1, 2, 3. The question *How do we acquire language?* can be restated as *How do we move from one rule to the next? From rule 3 to rule 4?* More generally, if i represents the last rule we have acquired, and $i + 1$ represents the next rule we are ready to acquire, how do we move from i to $i + 1$? The Input Hypothesis claims that we move from i to $i + 1$ by understanding input containing $i + 1$.

Reading Hypothesis   The reading version of the Input Hypothesis is the Reading Hypothesis. The Reading Hypothesis claims that much of our competence in literacy—our ability to read, to write, to spell, to recognize vocabulary, and to use and understand complex grammatical structure—comes from reading, especially reading that we do from genuine interest and for pleasure.

Affective Filter Hypothesis

Comprehensible input is necessary for language acquisition, but it is not enough. In addition, the acquirer must be open to the input. The *affective filter* is a mental block that prevents acquirers from fully utilizing what they hear and read. When the filter is strong, the acquirer may understand the input, but it will not reach the *language acquisition device.*

Universal, cultural, and individual factors probably determine the strength of the affective filter, but the classroom or acquisition can influence the filter in several ways. Individuals who lack self-esteem or who are anxious will have a strong filter. Classroom techniques that violate the principles of language acquisition also cause anxiety and thereby strengthen the filter. These techniques include forcing students to speak before they are ready, which

Harcourt Brace School Publishers

violates the Input Hypothesis, and excessive correction of errors, which encourages overuse of the Monitor.

The presence of the affective filter explains how two students can receive the same comprehensible input, yet one makes progress while the other does not. One student is open to the input, while the other is not.

APPLICATION OF THE THEORIES

Before presenting the details of application, we first have to ask whether we even need any special instruction in school to help students acquire a second language. Most people, in fact, will tell you that language classes are not necessary and that the best way to learn a language is to go to the country in which it is spoken.

For the beginner, however, this is not the best way. The Input Hypothesis explains why. Most of what the beginner hears outside the classroom is not comprehensible. The "outside world" is usually reluctant to provide second-language acquirers

Harcourt Brace School Publishers

with comprehensible input. In school, however, we can provide comprehensible input efficiently. In fact, we can define a language class as a place where students can get comprehensible input. This is the central function of the language class. Of course, once a language acquirer reaches the intermediate level, going to the country in which the language is spoken can help a great deal because much of the input the acquirer reads and hears will be comprehensible.

Beginning Levels
(PREPRODUCTION AND EARLY PRODUCTION)

Total Physical Response (TPR)   The Total Physical Response method, invented by James Asher, was a true breakthrough. The idea is simple. The teacher gives a command that involves an overt physical response, and the students obey the command. At first, the instructor also performs the action in the command, but eventually the students do it alone. Students are not required to speak at all. For example, the instructor says, "Stand up!" and stands up himself or herself, and the students stand up. Gradually, the commands get more complicated.

TPR works. The research on TPR is impressive, dating back to 1965. It works because it supplies comprehensible input and does not require language production. Input in TPR is made comprehensible by the total physical response of the teacher and students. Students understand what "stand up" means because they see the teacher standing up.

Thanks to the Input Hypothesis, which states that given enough input the necessary grammar is provided, TPR can be used flexibly. Activities such as teaching students magic tricks, doing exercises, and teaching dancing qualify as TPR because, in all cases, the teacher's movement provides the background knowledge or context that helps make the input comprehensible.

Natural Approach   The Natural Approach, invented by Tracy Terrell, is a method of supplying comprehensible input for the beginner. This is done with use of activities that center on topics of interest to the students. These could include games, tasks, discussions, and storytelling (by the teacher). The input is made comprehensible by means of pictures and other realia, physical movement (TPR), gestures, and appeal to the students' background knowledge, information the student has acquired through his or her primary language.

The Natural Approach is organized. The teacher uses a clear syllabus and lesson plans. The syllabus is based on topics and activities of interest to the students. Thus, a Natural Approach syllabus designed for young children will be different from one intended for older children or adults.

In Natural Approach classes, students are encouraged to speak but are not forced to. All responses are voluntary; no one is called on. The procedure follows the Input Hypothesis: Speech is a result, not a cause, of language acquisition. When students respond in the second language, their errors are not corrected. This procedure follows from the claim that the use of consciously learned rules is extremely limited.

Thus, spoken fluency and grammatical accuracy are allowed to emerge. Students feel no pressure to use language in production that is beyond their capacity. Students are never forbidden from speaking, however.

Natural Approach activities for students in early stages of second-language acquisition need not require any student verbal response at all. During this stage, which Terrell called the "prespeech" stage, TPR is used, as well as activities that combine TPR with pictures. The following exemplifies the technique. The goal of the lesson is to familiarize the students with school personnel.

Show the students pictures of the school staff and talk about each person; for example: "This is the principal, Mr. Gonzales. He works in the office. He is very nice." Point and gesture to convey meaning. Distribute pictures or photos among the students. Then ask, "Who has a picture of the school nurse? The gym teacher?" Collect pictures and place them in a pocket chart, and ask students to come up and point to a particular school staff member.

Note that students need not respond verbally to participate. In such a lesson, their focus is on learning the names of the staff members, but at the same time, they are acquiring vocabulary and grammar.

Here is another exercise that exemplifies the same technique. Students need not respond verbally, and they are learning something useful. Note how movement can be used in this example to help make input comprehensible:

Show students how they are to walk quietly in line to the place where they will be having lunch. Show them how to walk through the lunch line to buy their lunch or walk directly to the sitting area if they have brought lunch. Talk about table manners, modeling acceptable and unacceptable behavior. Show them how to pick up food wrappers and where they are to dispose of trash. Familiarize students with commands such as "Walk to the lunch tables" and "Line up."

Harcourt Brace School Publishers

Other activities at this stage could include taking students' pictures and making a composite, getting students to line up by height, and making a seating chart (Brown and Palmer, 1988).

Intermediate Levels
(SPEECH EMERGENCE AND INTERMEDIATE FLUENCY)

In the speech emergence stage, students begin to produce longer, more complex language. During this stage students will make many grammatical errors. These errors will disappear with more comprehensible input.

It is also quite likely that all students will not be at exactly the same stage at the same time. The Natural Approach handles this variation easily. In terms of comprehension, it is not necessary for every student to understand every word the teacher says. In a Natural Approach class, there will be so much input that even if a student understands a modest percentage of it considerable language acquisition will occur. In terms of production, students at different stages will respond according to their ability—some will respond nonverbally, some with single words and short phrases, and others with longer sentences.

In the speech emergence stage, students begin to produce longer, more complex language.

A good speech-emergence activity, such as planning a birthday party, allows the teacher to use a great deal of interesting input that is well-supported by context. Students can participate in the activity even with limited ability to produce language and at different stages of language production.

In all Natural Approach activities, students are not called on individually. Instead, *random volunteered responses* are used, which means that anyone in the class can respond without raising his or her hand and several students can respond at the same time. Random volunteered responses are not as orderly as traditional classroom behavior, but they are closer to real communication and reduce student anxieties considerably.

BEYOND
T P R
AND THE
NATURAL APPROACH

TPR and Natural Approach are beginning language teaching methods; they provide students with what Cummins calls "conversational" language. As most teachers know, limited-English-proficient students typically pick up conversational language successfully. TPR and Natural Approach will facilitate the development of conversational language and are thus very worthwhile, but they do not help the child acquire what Cummins has labeled "academic" language: the language of school and the language of science, business, scholarship, and politics. Not all children develop academic language.

There are three ways of developing academic language, and we should utilize all three ways.

1. Free Voluntary Reading

Reading, especially free voluntary reading (or "reading because you want to"), is a powerful means of developing literacy—including reading ability, writing style, vocabulary, spelling, and grammar.

Perhaps the most powerful way to stimulate an interest in reading is by reading stories aloud to students. Reading stories aloud works because it is comprehensible input and because it promotes an interest in reading. When students are absorbed in the story, they subconsciously acquire the special vocabulary and grammar of the written language, and, as every elementary school teacher knows, they become interested in books.

At the intermediate level, in-school free reading programs have had a great deal of success for both first- and second-language acquisition. One of the best-known programs is Sustained Silent Reading (SSR), in which students read for pleasure, without any accountability, for a few minutes each day. Students who participate in SSR programs that last a sufficient length of time (about an academic year) consistently outperform comparison students who participate in traditional programs with tests of reading comprehension and vocabulary (Krashen, 1993).

2. Sheltered Subject Matter

In sheltered subject matter teaching, intermediate second-language students are grouped for comprehensible subject matter instruction. These classes have two crucial characteristics:

- They are for intermediate-level students only. They are not for beginners because the input would be too difficult for beginners to understand. They are not for advanced second-language acquirers or native speakers. When these students are included, they tend to dominate discussion with the result being less comprehensible input for intermediate-level students. When all students are in the same linguistic boat, it is easier to keep the input comprehensible.

- They are subject matter classes. Students, if they are tested, are tested on language, not subject matter. This helps ensure that the focus will be on understanding messages, not on learning grammatical rules or on studying vocabulary lists. Research on sheltered subject matter teaching shows that students in these classes acquire as much or more of the second language as students in regular intermediate language classes, and they learn an impressive amount of subject matter as well (Krashen, 1991).

Free voluntary reading and sheltered subject matter teaching can be termed "direct" application of the principle of comprehensible input. Direct applications present comprehensible input in English. We can also help second-language acquirers with methods and techniques that are indirect but very powerful.

3. Using the First Language

The first language can be used to supply background knowledge, knowledge of the world and of the subject matter, which can help enormously in making English input more comprehensible. Here is an example of how this can work: Consider two limited-English-proficient students entering the fourth grade who are at approximately the same level in English. Student 1, who has been taught in her first language, has had an excellent background in math. Student 2 is very weak in math. In fourth grade, let us presume, math is taught only in English. Obviously Student 1 will do

Harcourt Brace School Publishers

much better in math than Student 2. Student 1 will not only learn more math, but she will also acquire more English. Student 2 will acquire neither math nor English.

Developing Literacy Through the First Language It is extremely efficient to develop literacy first in the student's first language; the transfer to English is rapid. To see this, consider this three-step argument:

(1) We learn to read by reading. There is good evidence that we learn to read by understanding the message on the page. This view, argued by Smith (1994) and Goodman (1982), is identical to the Input Hypothesis. While a small amount of phonics is useful in helping children understand the message on the page, most of our knowledge of phonics, Smith argues, is the result of knowing how to read, not the cause.

(2) If we learn to read by reading, it will be easier to learn to read a language we already understand.

(3) Once we can read, we can read. The ability to read transfers dramatically across languages, even if the writing systems are different. Not only is there evidence for transfer from Spanish to English, but there is also evidence for transfer from Chinese to English, Japanese to English, and Turkish to Dutch.

Another sense in which literacy transfers across languages is the ability to use language to solve problems. This includes discovering new ideas as the writer moves from draft to draft and reading selectively for information relevant to a problem one is trying to solve.

PRINCIPLES OF SUCCESSFUL PROGRAMS

If the principles presented here are correct, they suggest that successful programs for limited-English-proficient students have the following characteristics:

- Comprehensible input in English, in the form of ESL and sheltered classes. This provides comprehensible input directly.

- Subject matter teaching done in the first language without translation. This indirect help provides background information that makes the English that students read and hear more comprehensible. Methods that use the first language for concurrent translation are not effective in helping students acquire English (Legaretta, 1979; Fillmore, 1985). When a translation is available, the children do not attend to the input in the second language, and teachers do not have to try to make this input comprehensible.

- Literacy development in the first language, which transfers to the second language.

There is strong evidence supporting the validity of each of these characteristics. Studies showing that students who participate in programs that have these three characteristics do very well, at least as well as students in all-day English programs, and usually better (Krashen and Biber, 1988).

A fourth desirable characteristic is the continuation of primary language development. There are good practical reasons (e.g. international business), cognitive reasons (there is evidence that bilingualism may be beneficial for certain cognitive abilities), and a high level of competence in the first language contributes to a healthy sense of biculturalism, an avoidance of the state of "bicultural ambivalence," shame of the first culture and rejection of the second culture (Cummins, 1981).

Harcourt Brace School Publishers

LITERATURE and ESL

Why is it a good idea to focus on literature, especially in this era of hard-headed practicality? Through the study of literature, students will naturally be involved in activities that strongly promote language, literacy, and thinking. In other words, literature can promote both language and cognitive development.

A good literature program deals with topics and themes of both universal and local interest, themes that encourage students to think about basic ethical questions (How should we live? How should we treat each other?) and basic metaphysical questions (Why are we here?). In a good literature program, students

> *read*   novels, short stories, and poetry dealing with these topics.
>
> *listen*   to others tell stories and read stories aloud.
>
> *write*   about their own ideas and about their reactions to others' ideas.
>
> *discuss*   these ideas.

Reading makes enormous contributions to both language and cognitive growth. It is the source of our reading comprehension ability, writing style, and much of our spelling competence. While we get our basic vocabulary and grammar from listening to speech, much of our vocabulary and grammatical development after we reach school age comes from reading.

Reading also helps thinking. Reading is the major source of new ideas for many people. Those who read more, know more.

Listening makes a powerful contribution. Children who are read to regularly are superior in reading comprehension, vocabulary, and oral language ability. When children are read to, they begin to acquire the special language of writing, its particular grammar and vocabulary, as well as knowledge about how stories are put together (story grammar). This knowledge helps make their own reading much more comprehensible. As anyone who has read to children knows, reading aloud gets children "hooked on books." It leads to an interest in free voluntary reading, a habit that ensures continued literacy development.

Writing does not help in developing language and literacy. Those who write more do not necessarily write better. But writing makes a profound contribution to cognitive development. When we write our ideas down, we take thoughts that are vague and abstract and make them concrete. Writing is a powerful intellectual tool that helps us clarify our thinking and solve problems.

Discussion has the potential of helping certain aspects of language development because it can result in hearing new vocabulary and grammar. When teachers and students discuss stories, teachers are able to provide information that makes texts more comprehensible and to relate stories to students' experiences, which makes the text more interesting. In addition, discussion contributes to cognitive development. Just as is the case with writ-

Harcourt Brace School Publishers

ing, in discussion we often clarify our own ideas—in trying to express ourselves, our thoughts become clearer.

What should students read about, listen to, write about, and discuss? A good literature program supplies the answer—*ideas*.

Cause and Effect

Language development and cognitive development are a result of students' "wrestling with" ideas: reading about them, listening to them, writing about them, and discussing them. We don't first learn language and facts and then use them in the study of literature. Literature is the source of language and cognitive development.

Free Voluntary Reading

Well-taught literature programs instill in students a love of books and a desire to read on their own. Because free reading makes such a large contribution to the development of literacy, one can even claim that a successful literature program is one in which students are reading more independently.

WHAT ABOUT LITERATURE IN THE FIRST LANGUAGE?

Studying literature in a student's first language is not a luxury. There is good reason to believe it will help the student acquire English more rapidly and provide him or her with the knowledge and abilities necessary for success in the English-speaking mainstream. A good literature program in the primary language has these advantages:

Background knowledge—Students who study literature in their primary language will gain knowledge of the world as well as an understanding of what literature is. Good books and helpful, teacher-guided discussion can inform students about social studies and science. This knowledge helps make English input more comprehensible and thus accelerates English language development. In addition, a student who has participated in a good literature program in the primary language understands how to discuss and write about the ideas in a story, and has developed an appreciation of good literature. This makes the study of literature in English more comprehensible and more meaningful.

Literacy transfers—As noted earlier, developing literacy in one language facilitates the development of literacy in any other. In addition, there is every reason to hypothesize that those who read for pleasure in one language will read for pleasure in general.

FEATURES OF THE LESSON

The following before- and after-reading activities are choices for helping second-language students prepare to read and respond to the selections in the SIGNATURES READING PROGRAM. Only those activities that you think will be most helpful for your students should be completed.

Part I

Introducing the Literature

BUILDING BACKGROUND

Prior Knowledge

Helpful tips for tapping prior knowledge and developing concepts

TPR: Total Physical Response

Activities with suggested teacher movements that help make the input comprehensible

Develop Oral Language

A rhyme or chant introducing some of the concepts and words that students will encounter in the selection

BUILDING CONCEPTS

Poster

A four-color poster that can be used to stimulate discussion and provide comprehensible input

Rereading

An opportunity to reread the rhyme or chant for students who may benefit

Copying Master

A copying master that may be completed independently or with a partner

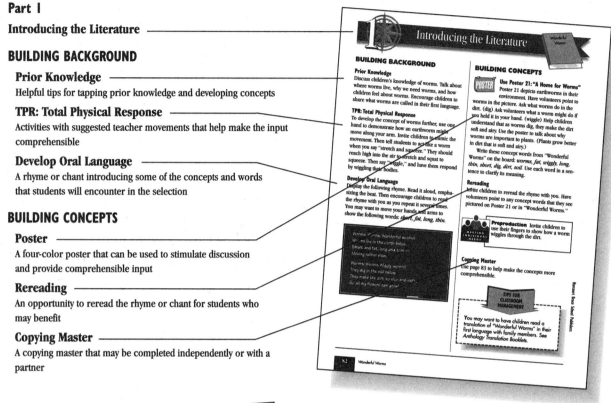

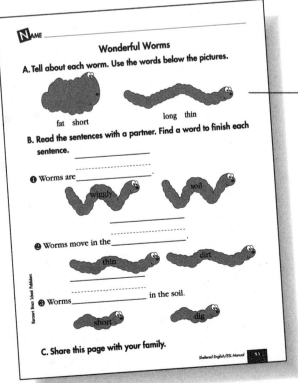

Copying Master

Fun activities that encourage the development of listening, speaking, reading, and writing and provide comprehensible input

Harcourt Brace School Publishers

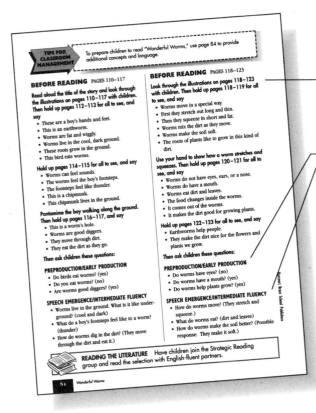

BEFORE READING

Take students on a "picture walk" through the selection before they read with Strategic Reading groups. The statements and leveled questions provided are suggestions and should not be used verbatim.

Preproduction/Early Production
Speech Emergence/Intermediate Fluency

Leveled questions to meet the needs of the students in your class

Part 2
Responding to the Literature

Comprehension Check

Examples of additional leveled questions to meet the needs of all second-language students in your group and to check comprehension

Additional Activities

Three additional activities that develop listening, speaking, reading, and writing skills

ESL/Title I Library

An opportunity for students to read a trade book in the ESL/Title I Library or an additional title that corresponds to the theme of the selection

School↔Home Connection

A suggestion for involving family members in a discussion of the selection and in the responding activities

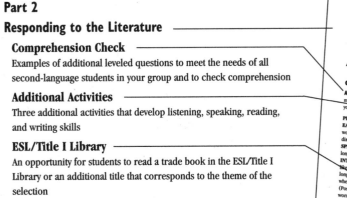

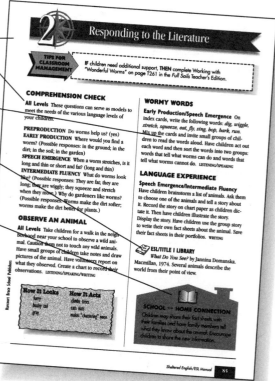

Harcourt Brace School Publishers

Introducing the Literature

Clap Your Hands

BUILDING BACKGROUND

Prior Knowledge

Talk with children about the names of different parts of their bodies. Name these body parts as you point to your own arms, hands, fingers, legs, feet, toes, head, and nose. Have children point to their own arms, hands, fingers, legs, feet, toes, head, and nose. Encourage them to say the names of the body parts in both English and their first language.

TPR: Total Physical Response

To further develop the concept of parts of the body, invite children to follow commands. Model each command as you give it. *Clap your hands. Stomp your feet. Shake your arms. Wiggle your toes. Touch your nose. Wiggle your fingers. Pat your head.*

Develop Oral Language

Display the following rhyme. Read the rhyme aloud, pantomiming actions and pointing to body parts and objects to emphasize the lines. Then invite volunteers to repeat the rhyme with you several times.

How are fingers like your toes?
Neither are on your nose!
How are hands like your feet?
They both can tap a beat.

How is a smile like a frown?
A smile is a frown upside down.
How is big like small?
Why, they're not alike at all!

BUILDING CONCEPTS

Use Poster 1: "All About Us"

Poster 1 shows the names of different body parts. Invite children to look at the two boys on the poster. Read aloud the labels with children, and ask volunteers to point to each boy's hands, feet, toes, and fingers. Ask which boy has a smile. (The boy with glasses) Ask which boy has a frown. (The boy without glasses) Ask who holds a small ball. (The boy without glasses) Use Poster 1 to help children develop their understanding of parts of the body.

Write these concept words from "Clap Your Hands" on the board. Read them aloud as you describe each one: *hands, feet, toes, fingers, big, small, smile, frown.*

Rereading

Invite children to reread the rhyme with you. Have volunteers point to any pictures on Poster 1 or in "Clap Your Hands" that describe the concept words.

MEETING INDIVIDUAL NEEDS

Extra Support Have partners trace outlines of their hands. Children can decorate the tracings and display them in the classroom.

Copying Master

Use page 3 to help make the concepts more comprehensible.

TIPS FOR CLASSROOM MANAGEMENT

You may want to have children read a translation of "Clap Your Hands" in their first language with family members. See *Anthology Translation Booklets.*

Harcourt Brace School Publishers

Clap Your Hands

A. With a partner, match each word to a picture.

frown

smile

hands

feet
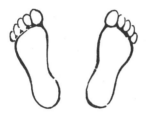

toes

fingers
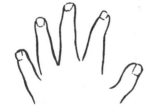

small

big

B. Try to do these things.

Tell what you can do with your hands, feet, toes, and fingers.

Tell what makes you smile and frown.

Name something big and something small.

C. Share this page with your family.

To prepare children to do a shared reading of "Clap Your Hands," use page 4 to provide additional concepts and language.

BEFORE READING PAGES 4–17
(or *Picture Perfect* pages 8–21)

Read aloud the title, and invite children to look at the illustrations on pages 4–17. Hold up pages 4–11, point to the pictures, and say

- These are children. These are animals.
- The children and animals are having fun.
- They clap their hands and stomp their feet.
- They shake their arms. They rub their tummies.
- They pat their heads and wiggle their toes.
- They stick out their tongues. They touch their noses.
- They roar and growl. They kiss.

Demonstrate some of the actions in the story. Then hold up pages 12–17, and say

- The children and animals wiggle their fingers.
- They slap their knees.
- They find something big.
- They spin around.
- They close their eyes and count to four.
- They do somersaults across the floor.

Then ask children these questions:

PREPRODUCTION/EARLY PRODUCTION

- Are the children and animals having fun? (yes)
- Do the children and animals do somersaults? (yes)
- Can you do a somersault? (yes/no)

SPEECH EMERGENCE/INTERMEDIATE FLUENCY

- What do the children and animals do with their hands? (clap)
- What parts of their bodies do they wiggle? (their toes and fingers)

BEFORE READING PAGES 18–32
(or *Picture Perfect* pages 22–37)

Look at the illustrations on pages 18–32 with children. Hold up pages 18–25, and say

- The children and animals act like clowns.
- They hop and flap.
- They are quiet. They say their names.
- They tell how old they are.
- They purr and bark. They crawl and jump.

Demonstrate some of the actions in the story. Then hold up pages 26–32, and say

- The children and animals count their fingers and toes.
- They wiggle their eyebrows and noses.
- They smile. They frown.
- They stand on one foot and jump.
- They fly like an airplane.
- They wave good-bye.

Then ask children these questions:

PREPRODUCTION/EARLY PRODUCTION

- Do the children and animals act like clowns? (yes)
- Can you hop like a bunny? (yes) Show me.

SPEECH EMERGENCE/INTERMEDIATE FLUENCY

- What do the children and animals tell each other? (their names, age)
- Can you name two things that the children and animals do in this story? (Accept any of the actions described.)
- Are the children and animals having fun? Why or why not? (Possible response: Yes, they are doing fun things.)

READING THE LITERATURE Have children join the Strategic Reading group and do a shared reading of the selection.

Harcourt Brace School Publishers

Responding to the Literature

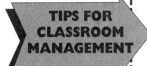
TIPS FOR CLASSROOM MANAGEMENT

IF children need additional support, **THEN** complete the Comprehension Check with them using the appropriately leveled questions. You may also want to have them participate in the Simon Says activity.

COMPREHENSION CHECK

All Levels These questions can serve as models to meet the needs of the various language levels of your children.

PREPRODUCTION Are there only animals in this story? (no) Are there children and animals in this story? (yes)

EARLY PRODUCTION Do the children and animals do things that are fun or things that are hard work? (things that are fun) Do they talk and move in this story or just talk? (talk and move)

SPEECH EMERGENCE What are some of the body parts that the children and animals use? (Responses will vary.) What do the children do with their feet? (Possible responses: stomp, wiggle toes, jump)

INTERMEDIATE FLUENCY What do you think is the silliest thing the children and animals do? (Responses will vary.) What other fun things could they do? (Responses will vary.)

ACT OUT THE STORY

All Levels Invite partners to choose an action in the story and draw a picture of themselves doing it. Then have partners demonstrate their action without telling their classmates what they are doing. Have their classmates find the page in the Big Book that shows the action. The partners can show their picture to confirm whether their classmates are correct. WRITING

SIMON SAYS

Early Production/Speech Emergence Lead a game of "Simon Says" in which children use hands, feet, toes, fingers, and other parts of their bodies to act out commands. After modeling how to lead the game, invite volunteers to take turns being the leader and calling out commands on their own. LISTENING/SPEAKING

WRITING A STORY

All Levels Invite children to create their own story in which children and animals have fun together. Suggest that they draw pictures showing the children and animals doing activities like those shown in the book. Ask children to write captions for their pictures. Assist students as needed. WRITING

ESL/TITLE I LIBRARY

Here Are My Hands by Bill Martin Jr. and John Archambault. Henry Holt, 1985. A dozen children point out and describe parts of their bodies. **Available on ESL/Title I Audiocassette.**

SCHOOL ↔ HOME CONNECTION
Ask children to take home their stories and share them with their family members. Encourage them to perform for their family members the actions they drew.

Harcourt Brace School Publishers

Introducing the Literature

The Itsy Bitsy Spider

BUILDING BACKGROUND

Prior Knowledge

Explore children's knowledge of spiders. Have them describe spiders. Help them recognize that a spider is an animal with eight legs. Then talk about where spiders live. Point out that many spiders spend much of their life in a web. If children know the song "The Itsy Bitsy Spider," encourage them to sing it. Invite children to say the word *spider* in their first language.

TPR: Total Physical Response

Use your fingers to demonstrate how a spider moves. Invite children to use their fingers to imitate the way in which a spider moves. Have them move their "finger spiders" by following your commands. Tell children to move their spiders across their desk, up their arm, and so on.

Develop Oral Language

Display the following rhyme, and read it aloud, emphasizing the rhyming words. Invite children to join you as you repeat the rhyme several times. You may want to point to the following illustrations in "The Itsy Bitsy Spider": spider, spout, tree, pail, wall, chair, web, rest.

> A spider can climb as high as can be.
> It can climb up a spout.
> It can climb up a tree.
> It can climb up a pail,
> Or a wall,
> Or a chair.
> It can make a soft web
> And rest
> In the air.

BUILDING CONCEPTS

POSTER

Use Poster 2: "Spider Facts"

Poster 2 shows the parts of a spider and the environments in which spiders live. Point to the spider and talk about it. Ask children to count with you the number of legs on the spider. Tell what the spider's home is called. (web) Help children name things a spider can climb. (spout, pail, chair, tree) Point out that spiders catch their food in webs. Discuss what else spiders do in webs. (rest)

Write these concept words from "The Itsy Bitsy Spider" on the board. Read them aloud and talk about each one: *spider, spout, pail, chair, tree, web, rest*.

Rereading

Invite volunteers to reread the rhyme with you. Encourage them to point to illustrations of concept words pictured in "The Itsy Bitsy Spider."

MEETING INDIVIDUAL NEEDS

Challenge Ask children to make lists of animals according to the number of legs they have.

Copying Master

Use page 7 to help make the concepts more comprehensible.

TIPS FOR CLASSROOM MANAGEMENT

You may want to have children read a translation of "The Itsy Bitsy Spider" in their first language with family members. See *Anthology Translation Booklets*.

Harcourt Brace School Publishers

The Itsy Bitsy Spider

A. Talk with a partner about spiders. Circle the things that a spider can climb.

spout   pail   chair

sun   rain   tree

B. Write a word that tells where a spider rests.

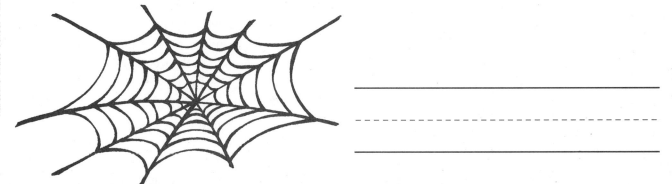

_____

- - - - - - - - - - - - - - - - - -

_____

C. Take this page home. Tell your family about spiders.

Harcourt Brace School Publishers

TIPS FOR CLASSROOM MANAGEMENT

To prepare children for a shared reading of "The Itsy Bitsy Spider," use page 8 to provide additional concepts and language.

BEFORE READING PAGES 6–17
(or *Picture Perfect* pages 40–51)

Read aloud the title, and look through the illustrations on pages 6–17 with children. Then hold up pages 6–10 for all to see, point to the appropriate pictures, and say

- This is a spider. This spider is small.
- This is a waterspout.
- The spider climbed up the waterspout.
- It rained. The spider was washed out.
- The sun came out. The rain dried.
- The spider climbed up the spout again.

As you hold up pages 11–14 for all to see, point to the appropriate pictures, and say

- Here is the spider. It climbed up a wall.
- The fan went on. The spider fell.
- The fan went off.
- The spider climbed up the wall again.

As you hold up pages 15–17 for all to see, point to the appropriate pictures, and say

- The spider climbed up a pail.
- A mouse came in and moved its tail.
- The spider fell down.
- The mouse ran away.
- The spider climbed up the pail again.

Then ask children these questions:

PREPRODUCTION/EARLY PRODUCTION
- Is this story about a cat? (no)
- Is the spider small or big? (small)
- Did the spider climb or dig? (climb)

SPEECH EMERGENCE/INTERMEDIATE FLUENCY
- What animal did the spider meet? (a mouse)
- What happened when the spider climbed the waterspout? (Possible responses: It rained; the spider was washed out.)

BEFORE READING PAGES 18–32
(or *Picture Perfect* pages 52–67)

Look at the illustrations on pages 18–32 with children. As you hold up pages 18–22 for all to see, point to the appropriate pictures, and say

- Here is the spider.
- The spider climbed up a chair.
- A cat jumped up. The spider fell off.
- The cat fell asleep.
- The spider climbed up the chair again.

Hold up pages 23–32 for all to see, and say

- Here is the spider.
- The spider climbed up a tree.
- The tree was wet. The spider fell.
- The spider landed near the child.
- The sun dried the tree.
- The spider climbed up to the top.
- The spider made a web.
- The spider rested.

Then ask children these questions:

PREPRODUCTION/EARLY PRODUCTION
- Did the spider climb a table? (no)
- Did the spider climb a chair? (yes)
- Did the spider climb a tree or a flower? (tree)

SPEECH EMERGENCE/INTERMEDIATE FLUENCY
- What animal does the spider meet in this part of the story? (a cat)
- What happened when the spider climbed the tree the first time? (The spider fell.)
- What happened when the spider climbed the tree the second time? (Possible responses: The spider climbed to the top; the spider made a web; the spider rested.)
- What do you think about this spider? (Possible response: It never gives up!)

READING THE LITERATURE Have children join the Strategic Reading group and do a shared reading of the selection.

Harcourt Brace School Publishers

Responding to the Literature

IF children need additional support, **THEN** complete the Comprehension Check with them using appropriately leveled questions. You may also want to have them participate in the Itsy Bitsy Song activity.

COMPREHENSION CHECK

All Levels These questions can serve as models to meet the needs of the various language levels of your children.

PREPRODUCTION Did the spider climb the waterspout again after it was washed out? (yes) Did the spider climb the tree again after it fell? (yes)

EARLY PRODUCTION Did the spider fall off the waterspout and the tree because they were wet or because they were too high? (wet) Did the spider rest or jump on the web? (rest)

SPEECH EMERGENCE What did the spider climb? (waterspout, wall, pail, chair, tree) What animals did the spider meet? (mouse, cat)

INTERMEDIATE FLUENCY What happened at the end of this story? (Possible responses: The spider climbed to the top of a tree; the spider made a web and rested.) Why do you think the spider rested? (Possible response: It was tired.)

SPIDER FOR A DAY

All Levels Have children work in small groups to pretend that they are a spider for a day. Ask them to draw or write about things that they would do. Then have the groups share their lists with each other. LISTENING/WRITING

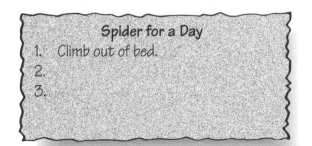

ITSY BITSY SONG

Early Production/Speech Emergence Point out that the words in this story are also the words to the song "The Itsy Bitsy Spider." Using the Big Book, point to the words as you sing the verses. Then sing the song again, and invite children to join you. Encourage children to add hand movements as they sing. LISTENING/SPEAKING

LANGUAGE EXPERIENCE

Speech Emergence/Intermediate Fluency Encourage children to write their own story about the Itsy Bitsy Spider. Brainstorm with them a list of other things that the spider could climb. As children dictate the story, record it on paper. Invite each child to choose his/her favorite story event and illustrate it. Display children's drawings along with the story in the classroom. WRITING

TRADE BOOK

Opposites by Sandra Boynton. Simon & Schuster, 1995. Children will enjoy learning opposites as they read this rhyme.

SCHOOL ↔ HOME CONNECTION
Invite children to share their drawings and retell the new spider story to their family members. Encourage them to ask family members what they know about spiders.

Harcourt Brace School Publishers

Introducing the Literature

The Earth and I

BUILDING BACKGROUND

Prior Knowledge

Talk with children about the Earth as home to all living things—people, plants, animals. Then discuss the importance of keeping the Earth clean. Talk about what might happen to plants and animals if the Earth gets dirty, or polluted. Invite children to tell about ways they can help keep the Earth clean.

TPR: Total Physical Response

Brainstorm with children ways in which they can help keep the Earth clean. Write the list on the board. Point to each item, and demonstrate the action. Then have children follow you as you model the actions and give directions. For example, as you pantomime picking up litter, you might say *We keep the Earth clean by picking up litter. We keep the Earth clean by recycling cans and bottles.*

Develop Oral Language

Display and read aloud the following rhyme. Then invite children to join in as you repeat the rhyme several times. You may want to point to the following in "The Earth and I": *Earth, backyard, play, apple tree, dirty, clean.* You can also use facial expressions to demonstrate the meanings of the words *sad* and *happy.*

> The Earth and I are friends,
> We're as close as we can be.
> We meet in my backyard
> and play near the apple tree.
>
> When the Earth is very dirty,
> I feel sad and blue.
> I help the Earth stay pretty and clean
> Then I feel happy—don't you?

BUILDING CONCEPTS

Use Poster 3: "Help the Earth"

Poster 3 contrasts a dirty and a clean Earth. Point to the first scene. Talk about why the friends look sad. Have volunteers tell what the Earth looks like in the backyard. (dirty) Point to the second scene and ask how the friends keep the Earth clean and pretty. (pick up litter, plant flowers to help clean the air, recycle) Talk about how the Earth and the friends look in the third picture. (clean; happy) Use Poster 3 to discuss how the children have helped keep the Earth clean.

Write these concept words from "The Earth and I" on the board. Read them aloud as you discuss each one's meaning: *Earth, friends, play, backyard, help, sad, happy.*

Rereading

Invite children to reread the rhyme with you. Encourage volunteers to say other sentences about the Earth.

MEETING INDIVIDUAL NEEDS

Preproduction Invite children to make a sad face and a happy face.

Copying Master

Use page 11 to help make the concepts more comprehensible.

TIPS FOR CLASSROOM MANAGEMENT

You may want to have children read a translation of "The Earth and I" in their first language with family members. See *Anthology Translation Booklets.*

Harcourt Brace School Publishers

The Earth and I

A. Work with a partner. Talk about the pictures. Use the words in the bin to help you.

happy   sad
friends   play
help   Earth
backyard

B. Talk about each picture. Write a word about each one.

_____   _____   _____

- -

_____   _____   _____

C. Share this page with your family.

To prepare children to do a shared reading of "The Earth and I," use page 12 to provide additional concepts and language.

BEFORE READING PAGES 5–19
(or *Picture Perfect* pages 70–85)

Read aloud the title. Call attention to the globe, and tell children it is a model of the Earth. Then look through the illustrations on pages 5–19 with children. Point to appropriate pictures on pages 5–13 for all to see as you say

- This is a boy.
- The boy and the Earth are friends.
- The boy goes for walks with the Earth.
- The boy talks to the Earth.
- The Earth listens to the boy.
- The boy listens to the Earth.
- The boy feels a raindrop.

Display pages 14–19 for all to see, and say

- The boy and the Earth are friends.
- The boy plays with the Earth.
- They play in the boy's backyard.
- The boy helps the Earth grow.
- The Earth helps the boy grow.

Then ask children these questions:

PREPRODUCTION/EARLY PRODUCTION

- Is this story about the moon? (no)
- Is this story about the Earth? (yes)
- Are the boy and the Earth friends? (yes)
- Do the Earth and the boy help each other grow? (yes)

SPEECH EMERGENCE/INTERMEDIATE FLUENCY

- Why do the boy and the Earth help each other? (They are friends.)
- Where do the boy and the Earth play together? (in the boy's backyard)
- What other things do the boy and the Earth do together? (Possible responses: walk together; listen to each other; help each other grow)

BEFORE READING PAGES 20–32
(or *Picture Perfect* pages 86–99)

Look through pages 20–32 with children. Then display pages 20–25 for all to see, and say

- The boy sings for the Earth.
- The Earth sings for the boy.
- The boy hears birds sing.
- The boy dances for the Earth.
- The Earth dances for the boy.
- The boy sees leaves dancing in the wind.

Pantomime the boy dancing. Use your hands to show how the leaves "dance" around the boy. Then display pages 26–32 for all to see, and say

- The Earth is sad.
- It is full of litter.
- The boy is sad, too.
- The boy helps clean up the Earth.
- The boy helps make the Earth beautiful.
- The Earth is happy.
- The boy is happy, too.

Then ask children these questions:

PREPRODUCTION/EARLY PRODUCTION

- Do the boy and the Earth sing and dance for each other? (yes)
- Does the litter make the Earth sad or happy? (sad)
- Does the Earth feel sad or happy when the boy cleans it? (happy)

SPEECH EMERGENCE/INTERMEDIATE FLUENCY

- What makes the Earth sad? (Possible response: when people make it dirty)
- What does the boy do to help the Earth? (He helps clean up the Earth.)
- How does the Earth feel after the boy helps it? (The Earth feels happy.)

READING THE LITERATURE Have children join the Strategic Reading group and do a shared reading of the selection.

Harcourt Brace School Publishers

Responding to the Literature

TIPS FOR CLASSROOM MANAGEMENT

IF children need additional support, **THEN** complete the Comprehension Check with them using appropriately leveled questions. You may also want to have them participate in the A Song for Earth activity.

COMPREHENSION CHECK

All Levels These questions can serve as models to meet the needs of the various language levels of your children.

PREPRODUCTION Do the boy and the Earth talk to each other? (yes) Does the boy like the Earth? (yes)

EARLY PRODUCTION Does the boy make the Earth happy or sad? (happy)

SPEECH EMERGENCE Who sings for the boy? (Possible responses: the Earth; the birds)

INTERMEDIATE FLUENCY How does the boy help the Earth grow? (Possible response: He plants and takes care of a garden.) How does the Earth help the boy grow? (Possible response: The Earth grows food that the boy eats.)

RULES FOR A CLEAN EARTH

All Levels Have children work in small groups to brainstorm a list of four or five rules that people should follow to help keep the Earth clean. Encourage children to write their rules using pictures, or have them dictate the rules to you. Invite groups to share their rules with one another. LISTENING/SPEAKING/READING/WRITING

Rules for a Clean Earth
1. Put papers in garbage can.
2. Plant flowers.

A SONG FOR EARTH

Speech Emergence/Intermediate Fluency
Write the following lyrics on the board, and recite them for children. Then invite them to sing the song to the tune of "Here We Go Round the Mulberry Bush." LISTENING/SPEAKING

All my friends keep the Earth happy,
Keep the Earth happy, keep the Earth happy.
All my friends keep the Earth happy,
*   so early in the morning.*
This is the way we clean the backyard, etc.
This is the way we plant some flowers, etc.

WRITING A STORY

Speech Emergence/Intermediate Fluency
Invite children to write their own story entitled "The Earth and I." Have them draw pictures to show ways that they help the Earth. WRITING

ESL/TITLE I LIBRARY
Anno's Counting Book by Mitsumasa Anno. HarperCollins, 1975. This book introduces the numbers 0–12. **Available on ESL/Title 1 Audiocassette.**

SCHOOL ↔ HOME CONNECTION
Suggest that children share their stories with family members. Children can report back about ways family members have helped the Earth.

Harcourt Brace School Publishers

Introducing the Literature

BUILDING BACKGROUND

Prior Knowledge

Discuss forms of transportation with children. Point out that people and things move from one place to another in many different ways. Invite children to name some of those ways, such as by car, bus, train, plane, or boat. Write the forms of transportation on the board as volunteers name them. Then invite children to say each word in their first language.

TPR: Total Physical Response

To develop further the concept of transportation, demonstrate the actions related to each of the forms of transportation listed on the board. Then invite children to pantomime using the forms of transportation as you name each one.

Develop Oral Language

Display the following rhyme, and read it aloud. Then have children join you in repeating the rhyme several times. You may want to point to the following illustrations in "Olmo and the Blue Butterfly": scooter, ground, skateboard, wheels, bike, street-car, track, airplane, sky, rocket, stars.

> I'm riding on a scooter.
> I push along the ground.
> I'm gliding on a skateboard.
> The wheels go round and round.
>
> I'm pedaling my bike.
> I ride to school and back.
> I hop onto a streetcar.
> We move along the track.
>
> I get on board an airplane.
> I fly up in the sky.
> I blast off in a rocket.
> The stars go whizzing by!

BUILDING CONCEPTS

 Use Poster 4: "How We Move"
Poster 4 displays various forms of transportation. Invite children to look at the poster and name the things that can move people or things. Ask children to point to something they have ridden on and say its name. Ask which things move on the ground, which move on water, and which move in the air.

Write these concept words from "Olmo and the Blue Butterfly" on the board: *scooter, skateboard, bike, streetcar, airplane, rocket.* Read them aloud. Use each one in a sentence.

Rereading

Reread the rhyme. Encourage volunteers to point to illustrations of concepts on Poster 4.

 Preproduction Take children outdoors to see various forms of transportation. Have children point to each one as you say the name.

MEETING INDIVIDUAL NEEDS

Copying Master

Use page 15 to help make the concepts more comprehensible.

TIPS FOR CLASSROOM MANAGEMENT

You may want to have children read a translation of "Olmo and the Blue Butterfly" in their first language with family members. See *Anthology Translation Booklets.*

Harcourt Brace School Publishers

Olmo and the Blue Butterfly

A. Follow the boy from his home to the moon. How does he get there?

airplane
bike
scooter

skateboard
rocket
streetcar

B. Share this page with your family.

To prepare children to do a shared reading of "Olmo and the Blue Butterfly," use page 16 to provide additional concepts and language.

BEFORE READING PAGES 6–17
or *Picture Perfect* pages 102–113

Share the title of the Big Book, and look through the illustrations on pages 6–17 with children. Then display pages 6–11 for all to see, and say

- This is Olmo. He is in bed.
- He sits up and rubs his eyes.
- He sees a blue butterfly.
- Olmo jumps up. Olmo follows the butterfly.
- The butterfly flies in the air.
- It flies high and low.
- Olmo hops on a scooter.
- He follows the butterfly.

Pantomime Olmo riding his scooter. Then display pages 12–17 for all to see, and say,

- Olmo rides on a skateboard.
- He follows the butterfly.
- Olmo jumps on a bike.
- He follows the butterfly.
- Olmo rides on a motorbike.
- He follows the butterfly.

Then ask children these questions:

PREPRODUCTION/EARLY PRODUCTION

- Is the boy in this story named Olmo? (yes)
- Does Olmo follow a bird? (no)
- Did you ever follow a butterfly? (yes/no)
- Does Olmo ride a bike? (yes)
- Do you know how to ride a bike? (yes/no)

SPEECH EMERGENCE/INTERMEDIATE FLUENCY

- How does the butterfly move from place to place? (It flies in the air.)
- How does Olmo move from place to place? (Possible responses: He rides on a scooter; he rides on a skateboard; he rides a bike; he rides a motorbike.)

BEFORE READING PAGES 18–31
or *Picture Perfect* pages 114–127

Look through the illustrations on pages 18–31 with children. Then display pages 18–23, and say

- Olmo hops on a streetcar.
- He follows the butterfly.
- Olmo jumps in a boat.
- He follows the butterfly.
- Olmo flies in an airplane.
- He follows the butterfly.

Then display pages 24–31 for all to see, and say

- Olmo flies in a chopper.
- He follows the butterfly.
- Olmo rides in a rocket.
- He follows the butterfly.
- Now Olmo is back in bed.
- The butterfly is always with Olmo.

Then ask children these questions:

PREPRODUCTION/EARLY PRODUCTION

- Does Olmo ever catch the butterfly? (no)
- Does Olmo ride in a boat or a car? (boat)
- Does Olmo ride in an airplane or a train? (airplane)
- Does Olmo ride in a truck or a rocket? (rocket)

SPEECH EMERGENCE/INTERMEDIATE FLUENCY

- What does Olmo ride in when he is on the water? (boat)
- What does Olmo ride in when he is in the air? (airplane, chopper, rocket)
- Where is Olmo at the end of the story? (He is back in bed.)
- Where is the butterfly at the end of the story? (Possible response: on Olmo's bed)

READING THE LITERATURE Have children join the Strategic Reading group and do a shared reading of the selection.

Harcourt Brace School Publishers

Responding to the Literature

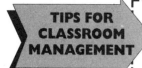

TIPS FOR CLASSROOM MANAGEMENT

IF children need additional support, **THEN** complete the Comprehension Check with them using appropriately leveled questions. You may also want to have them participate in the Be a Butterfly activity.

COMPREHENSION CHECK

All Levels These questions can serve as models to meet the needs of the various language levels of your children.

PREPRODUCTION Does Olmo follow an orange butterfly? (no) Does Olmo follow a blue butterfly? (yes)

EARLY PRODUCTION Does a scooter move on the ground or in the air? (on the ground)

SPEECH EMERGENCE What is on Olmo's bed at the end of the story? (the butterfly)

INTERMEDIATE FLUENCY Do you think Olmo was dreaming about the butterfly? Why or why not? (Responses will vary.) Have you ever followed a butterfly? (Responses will vary.)

A TRAVEL COLLAGE

All Levels Provide children with magazines, scissors, paste, and large sheets of paper. Have small groups find and cut out pictures that show different ways to travel. Ask children to paste the pictures on the paper to make a collage. Children who are able should write labels for the pictures. Encourage children to talk about the pictures they find. LISTENING/SPEAKING/WRITING

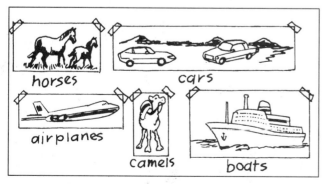

horses   cars   airplanes   camels   boats

BE A BUTTERFLY

Pre/Early Production/Speech Emergence
Invite children to follow you as you model actions and give "butterfly directions," such as the following:

Be a butterfly. Flap your wings.
Be a butterfly. Fly to the window.
Be a butterfly. Pretend you are landing on a flower.

After children follow your commands, encourage them to take turns giving "butterfly directions" of their own. LISTENING/SPEAKING

WRITING A STORY

Speech Emergence/Intermediate Fluency
Invite children to write their own stories in which they follow an animal, such as a bird or a bee. Have children draw pictures to show how they would follow the animal. Encourage them to write about the pictures they draw. WRITING

TRADE BOOK
Yes by Josse Goffin. Lothrop, Lee & Shepard, 1992. A man finds an egg and searches for its mother, only to find out it's not an egg at all.

SCHOOL ↔ HOME CONNECTION
Have children take home their stories and share them with their family members. Invite them to report back on how their family members liked their stories.

Harcourt Brace School Publishers

BUILDING BACKGROUND

Prior Knowledge

Discuss changes with children. Point out that when things change, they become different in some way. You might demonstrate by mixing food coloring into water or mixing two different paints to show a change in color. Discuss examples of changes with children, such as a kitten changing into a cat or a caterpillar changing into a butterfly. Invite children to name changes they have observed.

TPR: Total Physical Response

To develop further the concept of change, pantomime the act of changing. For example, you might pretend to be a caterpillar that changes into a butterfly. Encourage children to mimic you as you pantomime the actions. Then invite them to follow your directions and act out other changes that you describe.

Develop Oral Language

Display the following rhyme. Read it aloud, emphasizing the repeated verses. Then have children repeat the rhyme with you several times. You may want to point to the following illustrations in "An Egg Is an Egg": chick, hatches, egg, white, day, night, green, yard, snow, boy, baby.

> Look around you, and you'll find
> A change can happen any time!
>
> What is a chick before it hatches?
> An egg so smooth and white.
> What is the day before sunrise?
> The day was once the night.
> What is a green yard before spring comes?
> A yard with soft, white snow.
> What is a boy before he's a boy?
> A baby waiting to grow!
>
> Look around you, and you'll find
> A change can happen any time!

BUILDING CONCEPTS

Use Poster 5: "Changes"

Poster 5 shows examples of change. Invite children to look at the poster and point to specific things, such as the egg or something green. Then have children name the pairs of pictures. Ask how an egg changes. (It hatches.) Ask how a baby changes. (It grows.) Ask how the day changes into night. (Time passes. The Earth turns.) Ask how a green yard changes into a white yard. (It snows.)

Write these concept words from "An Egg Is an Egg" on the board, and read each one aloud: *egg, chick, change, green, white, day, night, baby, boy.* Use pictures to illustrate the meanings of unfamiliar words.

Rereading

Invite volunteers to join you in rereading the rhyme several times. Encourage them to talk about the illustrations on Poster 5.

MEETING INDIVIDUAL NEEDS

Challenge Have children name three ways that they have changed since they were babies.

Copying Master

Use page 19 to help make the concepts more comprehensible.

TIPS FOR CLASSROOM MANAGEMENT

You may want to have children read a translation of "An Egg Is an Egg" in their first language with family members. See *Anthology Translation Booklets.*

NAME _____

An Egg Is an Egg

A. Work with a partner. Label each picture.

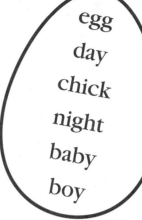

egg
day
chick
night
baby
boy

_____
- - - - - - - - - - - -
_____

_____
- - - - - - - - - - - -
_____

_____
- - - - - - - - - - - -
_____

_____
- - - - - - - - - - - -
_____

_____
- - - - - - - - - - - -
_____

_____
- - - - - - - - - - - -
_____

B. Color the pictures. Use green or white. Talk about the change.

C. Share this page with your family. Tell them how things change.

To prepare children to do a shared reading of "An Egg Is an Egg," use page 20 to provide additional concepts and language.

BEFORE READING PAGES 4–21

Read aloud the title of the Big Book. Then look through the illustrations on pages 4–19 with children. Hold up pages 4–9, and say

- This is an egg. The egg hatches.
- The egg becomes a chick.
- This is a branch. The branch breaks.
- The branch becomes a stick.
- Everything can change.
- The sun comes up. It is morning.

Point out that the picture on page 9 shows a house in the morning. Then display pages 10–14, and say

- A seed is planted.
- The seed grows to be a flower.
- Blocks are stacked.
- The blocks become a tower.

Point to the sun, and explain that the picture on page 15 shows a house during the day. Then display pages 16–21, and say

- Water is brewed. The water becomes tea.
- This is one person.
- Now there are two people.
- Two people call themselves "we."
- Everything can change.

Point to the setting sun, and explain that the picture on page 21 shows a house during the evening. Then ask children these questions:

PREPRODUCTION/EARLY PRODUCTION
- Can an egg change into a stick? (no)
- Can an egg change into a chick? (yes)

SPEECH EMERGENCE/INTERMEDIATE FLUENCY
- In the story, what can blocks change into? (a tower)
- What can water change into when it is brewed? (tea)

BEFORE READING PAGES 22–32

Look through the illustrations on pages 22–32 with children. Then display pages 22–27, and say

- The yard is green. It snows.
- The yard becomes white.
- It is day. The sun sets.
- The day changes to night.
- Everything can change.

Help children recognize that the picture on page 25 shows nighttime. Then display pages 28–32 for all to see, and say

- This is a baby.
- The baby grows.
- The baby becomes a boy.
- The mother loves the boy.
- He will always be her baby.
- Some things never change.

Then ask children these questions:

PREPRODUCTION/EARLY PRODUCTION
- Can a baby grow into a boy? (yes)
- Does snow make a yard white or green? (white)
- Is it day or night when the sun sets? (night)

SPEECH EMERGENCE/INTERMEDIATE FLUENCY
- What does the mother in this story tell the boy? (He will always be her baby.)
- What is something that changes? (Accept any response from the book or reasonable response drawn from personal experience.)
- What is something that never changes? (Possible response: A boy can always be his mother's baby.)

READING THE LITERATURE Have children join the Strategic Reading group and do a shared reading of the selection.

Harcourt Brace School Publishers

Responding to the Literature

TIPS FOR CLASSROOM MANAGEMENT

IF children need additional support, **THEN** complete the Comprehension Check with them using appropriately leveled questions. You may also want to have them participate in the Changing Game activity.

COMPREHENSION CHECK

All Levels These questions can serve as models to meet the needs of the various language levels of your children.

PREPRODUCTION Do people change? (yes) Do plants change? (yes)

EARLY PRODUCTION Can a seed change or does it always stay the same? (It can change.) Can a baby change or does a baby always stay the same? (A baby can change.)

SPEECH EMERGENCE What can an egg turn into? (Possible response: chick) Morning changes into afternoon. What does afternoon change into? (evening, night)

INTERMEDIATE FLUENCY What stays the same in this story? (The mother loves her little boy. He will always be her baby.) Which changes named in this book have you seen? (Responses will vary.)

AN ANIMAL CHART

All Levels Have children work in small groups to brainstorm a list of baby animals and the adult animals that these babies change into. Assist children as needed to record their ideas. Encourage children to illustrate their ideas. SPEAKING/WRITING

CHANGING GAME

Speech Emergence/Intermediate Fluency
Invite children to listen to riddles, such as the following, and guess the answers.

- I am a seed. What do I change into? (a plant)
- I am water in a freezer. What do I change into? (ice)

Invite children to work with a partner and make up riddles of their own. LISTENING/SPEAKING

WRITING ABOUT CHANGE

Speech Emergence/Intermediate Fluency
Invite children to draw pairs of pictures to show how things change. Encourage them to write what happens in each change. Help children bind their pages to make a book. WRITING

ESL/TITLE I LIBRARY
Have You Seen My Duckling? by Nancy Tafuri. Mulberry, 1984. When one of the ducklings strays from the nest, Mother duck asks for help. **Available on ESL/Title I Audiocassette.**

SCHOOL ↔ HOME CONNECTION
Invite children to take home the book to share with family members. Suggest that they ask family members to name other changes and report back their findings.

Harcourt Brace School Publishers

Bet You Can't

BUILDING BACKGROUND

Prior Knowledge

Talk with children about activities they can do by themselves, activities with which they need help, and activities they can't do. You may want to begin the discussion by saying: *Here's what I can and can't do. I can reach the top bookshelf. I can keep our room clean with your help. I can't lift a tree!* Invite children to give similar examples.

TPR: Total Physical Response

Help children write *can* and *can't* on two flashcards. Describe and demonstrate things you can do, such as lifting a chair or sharpening a pencil. Then describe and demonstrate things you can't do, such as touching the ceiling or moving a file cabinet. After several demonstrations, describe what you plan to do, and have children predict what you can and can't do by holding up the appropriate flashcard. Confirm their predictions by attempting to carry out your plan or demonstrating the action.

Develop Oral Language

Display the following rhyme, and read it aloud. Emphasize the words *can* and *can't* as you read. You might nod your head each time you read *can* and shake your head from side to side each time you read *can't*. Then have children repeat the rhyme with you several times.

> I can lift a basket,
> But I can't lift a car.
> I can clean my room,
> But I can't dust a star.
>
> I can go hiding,
> And you can go seek.
> But I bet you can't find me,
> Unless you peek!

BUILDING CONCEPTS

Use Poster 6: "Can or Can't?"

Poster 6 helps children focus on things they can and cannot do. Invite them to look at the first picture. Ask a volunteer to point to the basket. Ask who can lift the basket and who can't. (girl; boy) Draw attention to the second picture. Ask who can hide and who can't. (The boy can hide behind the chair. The girl can't hide behind the lamp.) Use Poster 6 to help children continue to talk about things they can and can't do.

Write these concept words from "Bet You Can't" on the board. Read them aloud as you point to each one: *can't, lift, can, hiding, clean, basket.* Use each word in a sentence.

Rereading

Invite children to join you in rereading the rhyme. Encourage them to point to any concept words pictured on Poster 6.

MEETING INDIVIDUAL NEEDS

Challenge Help children see that *can't* is a shortened form of *cannot.* Point out that the apostrophe takes the place of the missing letters.

Copying Master

Use page 23 to help make the concepts more comprehensible.

TIPS FOR CLASSROOM MANAGEMENT

You may want to have children read a translation of "Bet You Can't" in their first language with family members. See *Anthology Translation Booklets.*

Harcourt Brace School Publishers

Bet You Can't

A. Work with a partner. Talk about the pictures. Write *can* or *can't* to tell what the children can do or cannot do.

_____   _____   _____

- - - - - - - - - - - - -   - - - - - - - - - - - - -   - - - - - - - - - - - - -

_____   _____   _____

_____   _____   _____

- - - - - - - - - - - - -   - - - - - - - - - - - - -   - - - - - - - - - - - - -

_____   _____   _____

B. Take this page home. Tell your family what you can and can't do.

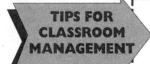

To prepare children to read "Bet You Can't," use page 24 to provide additional concepts and language.

BEFORE READING PAGES 44–54

Share the title, and look through the illustrations on pages 44–54 with children. Then display pages 46–50 for all to see, and say

- This is a boy. This is a girl.
- They are brother and sister.
- The boy asks what the girl is doing.
- She is cleaning up. It is bedtime.
- The boy says the girl can't lift the basket.
- The girl says she can.
- The girl lifts the basket.

Pantomime the girl lifting the basket and saying, "See. I can." Then hold up pages 51–54 for all to see, and say

- The boy says he can lift the basket.
- The girl says he can't.
- The boy tries. He falls.

Pantomime the boy trying to lift the heavy basket. Then ask children these questions:

PREPRODUCTION/EARLY PRODUCTION

- Can the girl lift the basket? (yes)
- Can the boy lift the basket? (no)
- Do you think you could lift the basket? (yes/no)
- Are the boy and girl brother and sister? (yes)

SPEECH EMERGENCE/INTERMEDIATE FLUENCY

- Why is the girl cleaning up the room? (It is bedtime.)
- What happens when the boy tries to lift the basket? (He falls.)
- Why do you think the girl can lift the basket but the boy can't? (Possible responses: The girl is bigger; the girl is stronger.)

BEFORE READING PAGES 55–66

Look through the illustrations on pages 55–66 with children. Then display pages 55–61, and say

- The girl is hiding.
- The boy starts to clean up.
- The girl says he can't.
- He can't because she is in the basket.
- The boy wants to get into the basket, too.
- The girl says they both can't get in it.
- The boy gets into the basket.

Hold up pages 62–66 for all to see, and say

- The boy starts to clean up again.
- The boy and girl work together.
- They clean up the room.

Then ask children these questions:

PREPRODUCTION/EARLY PRODUCTION

- Does the girl get into the basket? (yes)
- Does the boy get into the basket, too? (yes)
- Do the boy and girl work together at the end of the story? (yes)

SPEECH EMERGENCE/INTERMEDIATE FLUENCY

- Who gets into the basket first? (the girl)
- Who cleans up at the end of the story? (the boy and the girl)
- Do you think it is easier to clean up a room alone or with someone else? Why? (Possible responses: Working with someone else makes a job easier; work goes faster when someone else helps you.)

READING THE LITERATURE Have children join the Strategic Reading group and read the selection with English-fluent partners.

Responding to the Literature

TIPS FOR CLASSROOM MANAGEMENT

IF children need additional support, **THEN** complete Working with "Bet You Can't" on page T99 in the *Big Dreams* Teacher's Edition.

COMPREHENSION CHECK

All Levels These questions can serve as models to meet the needs of the various language levels of your children.

PREPRODUCTION Is this story about two children? (yes) Does the girl keep her toys in a basket? (yes)

EARLY PRODUCTION Who can lift the basket, the boy or the girl? (girl) Do the girl and the boy clean together or draw together? (clean)

SPEECH EMERGENCE When does this story take place? (at bedtime) What do the boy and girl say over and over again? ("Bet you can't." "Bet I can.")

INTERMEDIATE FLUENCY Why does the girl hide? (to get away from her brother) What does the girl keep in the basket? (Possible responses: her toys; books; a jump rope; a ball; roller skates; a stuffed rabbit; a quilt)

A BEDTIME LIST

All Levels Invite small groups of children to work together to make a list of things they do before they go to bed. Encourage groups to share their lists.
LISTENING/SPEAKING/WRITING

A Bedtime List
1. Clean up.
2. Brush teeth.
3. Read with Mom or Dad.
4. Say goodnight.

BET YOU CAN'T! CHALLENGE

Early Production/Speech Emergence Invite partners to challenge each other to do simple activities. For example, one partner might state, "Bet you can't lift the wastebasket." The other partner would then state, "Bet I can" and try to lift the basket. Make sure children do not challenge each other to perform dangerous activities. LISTENING/SPEAKING

WRITING A COMIC STRIP

Speech Emergence/Intermediate Fluency Call attention to the speech balloons in the story, and ask children to tell where else they have seen things written this way. (comic strips) Invite children to write their own comic strip about two children who work together to get something done. Have them draw pictures to illustrate the beginning, middle, and end. Then display the comic strips. WRITING

TRADE BOOK
Meow by Bernie Karlin. Simon & Schuster, 1991. A cat's constant meowing annoys a family until they learn the reason for all the noise.

SCHOOL ↔ HOME CONNECTION
Invite children to share their comic strips with their family members and to talk about things that are easier to do if they all work together.

Harcourt Brace School Publishers

Introducing the Literature

Little Elephant

BUILDING BACKGROUND

Prior Knowledge

Discuss children's knowledge of elephants. Help them recognize that an elephant is a very large animal with four legs, big ears, a tail, and a trunk. Point out that elephants are gray or brown with thick skin. They breathe and smell through their trunks and use their trunks to pick up things.

TPR: Total Physical Response

To help children understand elephants, pantomime an elephant moving slowly across the classroom. Use your arm as the elephant's trunk, and swing it back and forth as you walk. Demonstrate other ways an elephant moves and uses its trunk. Then invite children to imitate an elephant by following your directions. Give commands, such as *Swing your trunk* or *Lift up your trunk*.

Develop Oral Language

Display the following rhyme. Read it aloud, emphasizing the rhyming words. Then invite volunteers to repeat the rhyme with you several times. You may want to point to the following pictures in "Little Elephant": elephant, mother, splash, water, swing, trunk, bubbles.

> I am a little elephant.
> My mother lets me play.
> I splash in a pool of water.
> I swing my trunk this way.
>
> I make bubbles in the water.
> I feel so brave and strong.
> Then I look to see where Mother went.
> I've stayed away too long!

BUILDING CONCEPTS

Use Poster 7: "All About Elephants"

Poster 7 shows a mother elephant and her baby. Ask children to point to the elephant they think is the mother and tell why. (It is bigger.) Ask how many legs an elephant has. (four) Have volunteers name the part of an elephant that looks like a very long nose. (trunk) Then draw attention to the other elephants. Invite children to look at the pictures as you name ways that an elephant can use its trunk.

Write these concept words from "Little Elephant" on the board, and discuss each one as you point to it: *elephant, mother, water, splash, trunk, swing*.

Rereading

Invite children to reread the rhyme. Have them point to any concept words pictured on Poster 7.

MEETING INDIVIDUAL NEEDS

Speech Emergence Ask children where they might see elephants.

Copying Master

Use page 27 to help make the concepts more comprehensible.

TIPS FOR CLASSROOM MANAGEMENT

You may want to have children read a translation of "Little Elephant" in their first language with family members. See *Anthology Translation Booklets*.

Harcourt Brace School Publishers

Little Elephant

A. Read the words with a partner. Talk about the clues. Write a word after each clue. Put one letter in each box.

 trunk    mother    water

❶ She has a child.

☐ ☐ ☐ ☐ ☐ ☐

❷ Something you drink

☐ ☐ ☐ ☐ ☐

❸ Part of an elephant

☐ ☐ ☐ ☐ ☐

B. Talk with your partner about elephants.

Tell if you have ever seen an elephant.

Tell if you would like to ride on an elephant.

Tell how much you like elephants.

C. Take this page home, and share it with your family.

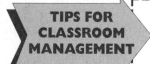

TIPS FOR CLASSROOM MANAGEMENT To prepare children to read "Little Elephant," use page 28 to provide additional concepts and language.

BEFORE READING PAGES 72–77

Read aloud the title. Then look through the photographs on pages 72–77 with children. As you display pages 72–74 for all to see, point to the appropriate photographs, and say

- This is a little elephant.
- This is the elephant's mother.
- The little elephant wants to play.
- It wants to play in the water.
- The mother lets the elephant play.

Display pages 75–77 for all to see, and say

- One toe goes into the water.
- Two toes go into the water.
- The little elephant makes a big splash.
- The elephant makes bubbles.
- The elephant lifts up its trunk.
- The elephant swings its trunk.
- The elephant goes under the water.

Then ask children these questions:

PREPRODUCTION/EARLY PRODUCTION

- Is this story about a little tiger? (no)
- Is this story about a little elephant? (yes)
- Does the little elephant want to play on the rocks or in the water? (in the water)

SPEECH EMERGENCE/INTERMEDIATE FLUENCY

- What part of the elephant goes into the water first? (toes)
- Who is with the little elephant? (its mother)
- What does the little elephant do in the water? (Possible responses: It splashes; it makes bubbles; it lifts its trunk; it swings its trunk.)

BEFORE READING PAGES 78–83

Look at the photographs on pages 78–83 with children. Then display pages 78–79, and say

- Can you see the elephant?
- Here is the elephant!
- It is time to get out.

Display pages 80–83 for all to see, and say

- Getting out is hard work.
- The elephant falls.
- The elephant tries again.
- The elephant gets out of the water.
- The elephant is in a hurry.
- The elephant looks for its mother.
- Mother is waiting!

Then ask children these questions:

PREPRODUCTION/EARLY PRODUCTION

- Does the little elephant get out of the water? (yes)
- Does the little elephant find its mother? (yes)
- Does the little elephant like the water? (yes)
- Do you like to play in the water? (yes/no)

SPEECH EMERGENCE/INTERMEDIATE FLUENCY

- What happens when the little elephant first tries to get out of the water? (It falls.)
- Who is waiting for the little elephant when it gets out of the water? (Mother elephant)
- What do you think the little elephant would say at the end of the story if it could talk? (Responses will vary.)

Harcourt Brace School Publishers

READING THE LITERATURE Have children join the Strategic Reading group and read the selection with English-fluent partners.

Responding to the Literature

TIPS FOR CLASSROOM MANAGEMENT

IF children need additional support, **THEN** complete Working with "Little Elephant" on page T139 in the *Big Dreams* Teacher's Edition.

COMPREHENSION CHECK

All Levels These questions can serve as models to meet the needs of the various language levels of your children.

PREPRODUCTION Is this story about a real elephant? (yes)

EARLY PRODUCTION Does the elephant want to play or sleep? (play) Is the elephant afraid of water or does it like the water? (It likes the water.)

SPEECH EMERGENCE What do you think the mother does when the little elephant is in the water? (Responses will vary.)

INTERMEDIATE FLUENCY How do you know that the mother elephant cares about the little elephant? (Possible responses: She lets him play; she waits for him while he is playing; she watches over him.) Have you ever seen an elephant in a zoo, in a movie, or on television? What did that elephant do? (Responses will vary.)

LITTLE ELEPHANTS

All Levels Invite children to work in pairs to brainstorm a list of things they can do as little elephants. Children can use drawings to record some of their ideas. Ask volunteers to read aloud their lists. LISTENING/SPEAKING/WRITING

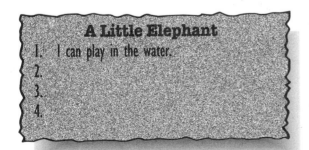

A Little Elephant
1. I can play in the water.
2.
3.
4.

CAN I BE AN ELEPHANT?

Early Production/Speech Emergence Provide the following statement and question as a model: *I have a trunk. Can I be an elephant?* Then invite children to ask each other questions, such as *I have feathers. Can I be an elephant?* or *I have four legs. Can I be an elephant?* LISTENING/SPEAKING

LANGUAGE EXPERIENCE

Speech Emergence/Intermediate Fluency Work with children to write a story about another baby animal that lives in a zoo. As individuals volunteer sentences, record them on chart paper. Read the story aloud with students. You may want to copy the story and have children illustrate it. WRITING

TRADE BOOK
Little Bird by Saviour Pirotta. William Morrow, 1992. Little Bird finds out that it can't wriggle like a worm or roll like a pig, but what it *can* do is fly.

SCHOOL ↔ HOME CONNECTION
Invite children to take home their stories and share them with their family members. Ask them to report back on how their family members liked the stories they wrote.

Harcourt Brace School Publishers

Introducing the Literature

Flower Garden

BUILDING BACKGROUND

Prior Knowledge

Write the word *flowers* on the board, and read it aloud. Encourage children to describe different flowers. Point out that flowers are often grown from seeds. Help children recognize that people can also buy plants that are already flowering.

TPR: Total Physical Response

Read aloud and demonstrate the following finger play. Have children do the motions with you.

I plant the red and yellow flowers in the flower bed.
   (Pretend to put seeds in the palm of your hand.)
The daisy opens its petals wide. *(Place wrists together with palms pointed up and fingers open.)*
The tulip bows its head. *(Place wrists together with palms pointed downward and fingers closed.)*

Develop Oral Language

Display the following rhyme, and read it aloud. Then invite children to repeat the rhyme with you several times. You can use pictures in "Flower Garden" to help children visualize the words *box, flowers, store, stairs, door, window, street.*

I'll buy a box of flowers.
I'll get them at the store.
I'll carry them right up the stairs,
To my apartment door.

I'll make a window garden
With colors bright and gay.
Then all the people on the street
Will look and smile today.

BUILDING CONCEPTS

POSTER

Use Poster 8: "Flower Gardens"

Poster 8 shows flowers grown in boxes. Invite children to point to the stairs, a door, a window, and the flowers. Say the colors of the flowers aloud, and have volunteers repeat them. Ask which flowers are near the stairs. (the purple and red flowers) Ask which flowers are above the door. (yellow, pink) Ask which are at the top windows. (orange, white)

Write these concept words from "Flower Garden" on the board. Say each one aloud, and use it in a sentence to clarify meaning: *flower, box, stairs, door, window, street, color.*

Rereading

Reread the rhyme with children as they point to any illustrated concept words on Poster 8.

MEETING INDIVIDUAL NEEDS

Challenge Encourage children to draw a flower and name these parts: *petals, stem, leaves.*

Copying Master

Use page 31 to help make the concepts more comprehensible.

TIPS FOR CLASSROOM MANAGEMENT

You may want to have children read a translation of "Flower Garden" in their first language with family members. See *Anthology Translation Booklets.*

Harcourt Brace School Publishers

Flower Garden

A. Talk about the picture with a partner. Write words to tell about the picture. Use the words in the flower garden.

flower   street   stairs   door   window   box

B. Color the flowers.

C. Share this page with your family.

TIPS FOR CLASSROOM MANAGEMENT

To prepare children to do a shared reading of "Flower Garden," use page 32 to provide additional concepts and language.

BEFORE READING PAGES 90–107

Read the title, and look through the illustrations on pages 90–107 with children. Then hold up pages 90–99 for all to see, and say

- This is a girl. She is at a store.
- She is with her father.
- The girl puts flowers in a shopping cart.
- The girl and her father pay for the flowers.
- Now the flowers are in a cardboard box.
- The girl and her father walk to the bus.
- They ride on the bus with the flowers.
- People on the bus see the flowers.

Hold up pages 100–107 for all to see, and say

- The girl carries the flowers.
- She goes up the stairs. She stops at each floor.
- The flowers are heavy.
- The girl gets to her front door.
- The girl and her father put paper on the floor.
- They get dirt for the flowers.
- They plant the flowers in a box.
- Each flower is a pretty color.

Then ask children these questions:

PREPRODUCTION/EARLY PRODUCTION

- Does the girl buy toys at the store? (no)
- Does the girl buy flowers at the store? (yes)
- Does the girl take the flowers to a park or to her home? (to her home)

SPEECH EMERGENCE/INTERMEDIATE FLUENCY

- How do the girl and her father get home from the store? (by bus)
- Why do you think the girl and her father put paper on the floor? (Possible response: so the dirt won't get on the floor)

BEFORE READING PAGES 108–120

Look through the illustrations on pages 108–120 with children. Then hold up pages 108–115 for all to see, and say

- Father puts the flowers in a box outside the window.
- The girl watches.
- The box is high above the street.
- People are on the street.
- They look up. They see the flowers.
- They see nice colors.
- The girl can see the street.
- Her mother is coming home.

Hold up pages 116–120 for all to see, and say

- This is a birthday cake. It has candles.
- There is chocolate ice cream, too.
- Mother comes in.
- The girl says, "Happy birthday!"
- It is Mother's birthday.
- The flowers are a present for her.
- The flowers look pretty in the window.

Then ask children these questions:

PREPRODUCTION/EARLY PRODUCTION

- Are the flowers a present for Father? (no)
- Are the flowers a present for Mother? (yes)
- Who puts the box in the window, the girl or her father? (her father)

SPEECH EMERGENCE/INTERMEDIATE FLUENCY

- What does the girl have for her mother when she gets home? (Possible responses: cake, ice cream, flowers)
- What does the girl say when her mother gets home? ("Happy birthday!")
- Which flower in the box do you like best? Why? (Responses will vary.)

READING THE LITERATURE Have children join the Strategic Reading group and do a shared reading of the selection.

Responding to the Literature

TIPS FOR CLASSROOM MANAGEMENT

IF children need additional support, **THEN** complete the Comprehension Check with them using appropriately leveled questions. You may also have them participate in the Flower Colors activity.

COMPREHENSION CHECK

All Levels These questions can serve as models to meet the needs of the various language levels of your children.

PREPRODUCTION Is this story about a boy? (no) Is this story about a girl? (yes)

EARLY PRODUCTION Is it Mother's or Father's birthday? (Mother's) Does the girl make a flower garden or a special drawing? (flower garden)

SPEECH EMERGENCE Where does the girl get the flowers? (at the store) What colors are the flowers? (Possible responses: purple, white, yellow, red)

INTERMEDIATE FLUENCY Do you think Mother is surprised when she gets home? Why or why not? (Possible response: Yes, she looks surprised in the picture.)

A BIRTHDAY CARD FOR MOTHER

All Levels Have children work with partners to make a birthday card. Show them how to fold a piece of paper in half to make a card. Suggest that children draw a picture on the front of the card and write a birthday message inside. Then have children display their cards and read their messages. LISTENING/SPEAKING/READING/WRITING

Happy Birthday, Mother, I hope you like the flowers. Love, Ariel

FLOWER COLORS

Preproduction/Early Production Play a word game with children. Give them the names and colors of flowers, and have them find examples of each color in the classroom. Encourage children to respond orally, for example: *I am a red rose. Name something else that is red.* (The ball is red.) Preproduction level children can point to objects in the classroom. LISTENING/SPEAKING

LANGUAGE EXPERIENCE

Speech Emergence/Intermediate Fluency Invite children to create their own stories about a birthday party for a family member. Suggest that children illustrate the stories, and encourage them to write what happens. Children can show their pictures and read their stories aloud. LISTENING/ SPEAKING/READING/WRITING

ESL/TITLE I LIBRARY
Window by Jeannie Baker. Greenwillow, 1991. Children can take a look at a man's life from boyhood to adulthood through pictures.

SCHOOL ↔ HOME CONNECTION
Invite children to share their stories with their family members. Encourage them to ask family members about favorite birthday presents they have received.

Harcourt Brace School Publishers

Introducing the Literature

Five Little Ducks

BUILDING BACKGROUND

Prior Knowledge

Invite volunteers to count from one to five in their first language. Then count from one to five in English. Have volunteers repeat the counting with you. Next, count backwards from five to one. Have volunteers repeat the backward counting.

TPR: Total Physical Response

To further develop children's understanding of numbers from one to five, give each child five counters. Ask children to pretend that the counters are ducks and that the surface of their desks is a pond. Then give directions and model the actions with counters. For example, you might say, "All five ducklings are together. One baby duck swims away."

Develop Oral Language

Display the following rhyme, and read it aloud. Emphasize the number words. Then have children repeat the rhyme with you several times. You can hold up fingers on one hand as you count to help children understand the number words.

> One, two, three, four, five—
>   Five little ducks that dip and dive.
> Five, four, three, two, one—
>   Five little ducks swimming just for fun.
> Five little ducks paddle out and back.
>   Five little ducks and five loud quacks!

BUILDING CONCEPTS

Use Poster 9: "Counting"

Poster 9 provides groups for children to count. Ask children to point to the ducks. Talk about what the ducks are doing. Point to the trees in the picture. Have children count them with you as you point to each one. Point to the frogs. Count them with children. Ask them to find and count other groups pictured on Poster 9.

Write these concept words from "Five Little Ducks" on the board. Read them aloud as you point to each one: *swimming, ducks, five, four, three, two, one.* Draw pictures or use pantomime to help children understand the words' meanings.

Rereading

Invite children to reread the rhyme with you. Have them point to any concept words pictured on Poster 9.

Preproduction As you count from 1 to 5, hold up five books, one at a time.

Copying Master

Use page 35 to help make the concepts more comprehensible.

TIPS FOR CLASSROOM MANAGEMENT

You may want to have students read a translation of "Five Little Ducks" in their first language with family members. See *Anthology Translation Booklets.*

Harcourt Brace School Publishers

Five Little Ducks

A. Count the ducks with a partner. Write the number under each picture.

B. Share this page with your family.

Harcourt Brace School Publishers

TIPS FOR CLASSROOM MANAGEMENT

To prepare children to read "Five Little Ducks," use page 36 to provide additional concepts and language.

BEFORE READING PAGES 124–129

Read the title, and have children look at pages 124–129. Hold up pages 126–127, and say

- Here are five little ducks.

Point to each one as you count aloud.

- They swam over the hills and far away.
- This is the mother duck.
- She said, "Quack, quack, quack, quack."
- Only four little ducks came back.

Point to each one as you count aloud.

- One little duck walked away.
- The duck went to the fox's house.

Hold up pages 128–129, and say

- Here are four little ducks.

Point to each one as you count aloud.

- They went swimming.
- Mother duck said, "Quack, quack, quack, quack."
- Only three little ducks came back.

Point to each one as you count aloud.

- One little duck walked away.
- This is the fox.
- The duck went to the fox's house.

Then ask children these questions:

PREPRODUCTION/EARLY PRODUCTION

- Is this story about ducks? (yes)
- Did the ducks go swimming? (yes)

SPEECH EMERGENCE/INTERMEDIATE FLUENCY

- How many little ducks were there at the beginning of this story? (five)
- What happened each time the little ducks went swimming over the hills and far away? (One of them did not come back.)

BEFORE READING PAGES 130–138

Look at the illustrations on pages 130–138 with children. As you hold up pages 130–133, say

- Here are three little ducks.

Point to each one as you count aloud.

- They swam over the hills and far away.
- Only two little ducks came back.

Point to each one as you count aloud.

- One little duck walked away.
- It went to the fox's house.
- Here are two little ducks.

Point to each one as you count aloud.

- They swam over the hills and far away.
- Only one little duck came back.
- The other duck went to the fox's house.

Hold up pages 134–138, and say

- Here is one little duck.
- The one little duck swam over the hills.
- The one little duck went to the fox's house and found the other ducks.
- The one little duck brought the other ducks home.
- Here are five little ducks with their mother.

Then ask children these questions:

PREPRODUCTION/EARLY PRODUCTION

- Did the little ducks come back home again? (yes)
- Did the mother duck find the little ducks? (no)

SPEECH EMERGENCE/INTERMEDIATE FLUENCY

- Were you worried about the ducks? Why? (Yes. The fox might eat them.)
- How many little ducks were there at the end of the story? (five)

READING THE LITERATURE Have children join the Strategic Reading group and read the selection with English-fluent partners.

Responding to the Literature

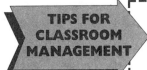

TIPS FOR CLASSROOM MANAGEMENT

IF children need additional support, **THEN** complete Working with "Five Little Ducks" on page T229 in the *Big Dreams* Teacher's Edition.

COMPREHENSION CHECK

All Levels These questions can serve as models to meet the needs of the various language levels of your children.

PREPRODUCTION Is this story about three little ducks? (no)

EARLY PRODUCTION Did the little ducks leave one by one or all at one time? (one by one)

SPEECH EMERGENCE What happened each day when the ducks went swimming? (One didn't return.)

INTERMEDIATE FLUENCY If the mother duck could talk, what do you think she would say to the little ducks at the end of the story? (Possible response: You should never go away by yourself.)

SAFETY RULES

All Levels Have children work in small groups. Invite them to brainstorm a list of safety rules for little ducks. You may want to suggest a rule, such as *Never go away by yourself.* Have children share their rules aloud. Record their ideas on chart paper. LISTENING/SPEAKING/WRITING

Rules for Ducks
1. Never go away by yourself.
2. Always swim in a group.
3. Never swim too far away.
4. Never talk to strange foxes.
5. Never go to a fox's house.
6. Always tell Mother where you are going.

DUCK MATH

Preproduction/Early Production/Speech Emergence Give children word problems, and invite them to work with a partner to find the answers. You may wish to provide children with counters to help them. Model word problems, such as *There are four little ducks. One swims away. How many are left? (three)* Have children make up their own problems to ask each other. LISTENING/SPEAKING

WRITING STORIES

Speech Emergence/Intermediate Fluency Invite children to write their own story about five little animals, such as five little kittens or five little birds. Encourage children to tell about how one little animal leaves the group each day. Have children illustrate the story and then share it with their classmates. LISTENING/READING/WRITING

TRADE BOOK
The Picnic by Emily Arnold McCully. Harper-Collins, 1984. This is a wordless picture book about a mouse who gets lost on the way to a family picnic.

SCHOOL ↔ HOME CONNECTION
Encourage children to take home their stories and share them with their families. Have them report back about how family members liked the stories.

Introducing the Literature

Little Gorilla

BUILDING BACKGROUND

Prior Knowledge
Talk with children about some of the wild animals that live in Africa. Help children name African animals—for example, monkey, lion, hippo, and giraffe. Invite volunteers to name the animals in both English and their native language.

TPR: Total Physical Response
To develop this concept further, pretend to be each one of the animals named by the children. Imitate the animals with both actions and noises. Then invite children to imitate each of the animals you name.

Develop Oral Language
Display the following rhyme, and read it aloud, emphasizing the rhyming words. Then have children repeat the rhyme with you several times. You may want to point to the following illustrations in "Little Gorilla": gorilla, parrot, monkey, trees, lion, hippo, giraffe.

I am a little gorilla.
  I live out in the wild.
I have many animal friends.
  I'm such a lucky child!
Green Parrot and Red Monkey
  Watch me from the trees.
Lion, Hippo, and tall Giraffe
  All take care of me.
My grandma, aunts, and uncles
  Say they love me true.
When I grow up, I hope they'll like
  A BIG gorilla, too.

BUILDING CONCEPTS

Use Poster 10: "African Animals"
Poster 10 shows African animals. Ask children to point to the parrot and the monkey. Point to the gorilla and have volunteers identify it by name. Point to the other animals in turn, and have children name them. Ask if anyone knows the full name for a hippo. (hippopotamus) Then invite volunteers to tell anything they know about the animals pictured, such as how they move or what they eat. Use Poster 10 to help children continue their discussion of African animals.

Write these concept words from "Little Gorilla" on the board. Read each word aloud, and talk about it: *gorilla, parrot, monkey, giraffe, lion, hippo.*

Rereading
Invite children to reread the rhyme with you. Have them point to any illustrations of concept words pictured on Poster 10.

Speech Emergence Have children refer to the list of concept words. Ask them to name two animals that are most alike. (gorilla, monkey)

MEETING INDIVIDUAL NEEDS

Copying Master
Use page 39 to help make the concepts more comprehensible.

TIPS FOR CLASSROOM MANAGEMENT

You may want to have children read a translation of "Little Gorilla" in their first language with family members. See *Anthology Translation Booklets.*

Harcourt Brace School Publishers

Little Gorilla

A. Work with a partner. Name the animals. Make a name tag for each animal. Use the words in the box.

giraffe	gorilla	hippo	lion	monkey	parrot

B. Share this page with your family.

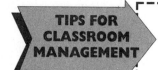

TIPS FOR CLASSROOM MANAGEMENT   To prepare children to read "Little Gorilla," use page 40 to provide additional concepts and language.

BEFORE READING PAGES 144–155

Share the title, and then look at the illustrations on pages 144–155 with children. Hold up pages 144–149, and say

- This is Little Gorilla.
- His mother loved him.
- His grandma and grandpa loved him.
- His aunts and uncles loved him.
- His father loved him.
- His whole family loved him.

Hold up pages 150–155, and say

- Pink Butterfly loved Little Gorilla.
- Green Parrot loved Little Gorilla.
- Red Monkey loved Little Gorilla.
- Big Boa Constrictor thought Little Gorilla was nice.
- Giraffe helped Little Gorilla.
- Young Elephant and Old Elephant came to see Little Gorilla.
- Lion roared for Little Gorilla.
- Old Hippo took Little Gorilla everywhere.
- Everybody in the forest loved Little Gorilla.
- One day something happened.

Then ask children these questions:

PREPRODUCTION/EARLY PRODUCTION

- Is this story about a little elephant? (no)
- Is Little Gorilla loved by everybody or just his family? (everybody)

SPEECH EMERGENCE/INTERMEDIATE FLUENCY

- What animals loved Little Gorilla? (other gorillas, a butterfly, a parrot, a monkey, a snake, a giraffe, elephants, a lion, a hippo)
- What do you think happened to Little Gorilla? (Accept all reasonable responses.)

BEFORE READING PAGES 156–164

Look at the illustrations on pages 156–164 with children. Then hold up pages 156–159, and say

- Little Gorilla began to grow and grow and grow.
- He got very big!

Hold up pages 160–164, and say

- The animals had a birthday party for Little Gorilla.
- Everybody came.
- Everybody sang.
- Everyone said, "Happy Birthday, Little Gorilla!"
- Little Gorilla was big.
- But everybody still loved him.

Then ask children these questions:

PREPRODUCTION/EARLY PRODUCTION

- Did Little Gorilla start to grow? (yes)
- Did the animals have a birthday party for Little Gorilla? (yes)
- Did the animals still love Little Gorilla? (yes)

SPEECH EMERGENCE/INTERMEDIATE FLUENCY

- What happened to Little Gorilla in this story? (He got big.)
- How was Little Gorilla different at the end of the story? How was he the same? (Possible responses: He was bigger; everybody still loved him; he still had all his friends and family.)
- What would you say at the end of the story if you were Little Gorilla? (Possible responses: It's nice to be big; I'm glad everybody still loves me; I like my birthday party.)

READING THE LITERATURE   Have children join the Strategic Reading group and read the selection with English-fluent partners.

40   *Little Gorilla*

Harcourt Brace School Publishers

TIPS FOR CLASSROOM MANAGEMENT

IF children need additional support, **THEN** complete Working with "Little Gorilla" on page T281 in the *Big Dreams* Teacher's Edition.

COMPREHENSION CHECK

All Levels These questions can serve as models to meet the needs of the various language levels of your children.

PREPRODUCTION Is Little Gorilla loved when he is small and when he is big? (yes)

EARLY PRODUCTION Does Little Gorilla live by himself or with a family of gorillas? (a family) Does Little Gorilla just know gorillas or does he know other animals, too? (other animals)

SPEECH EMERGENCE Where does Little Gorilla live? (in a forest) How does Little Gorilla change? (Possible responses: He grows up; he gets big.)

INTERMEDIATE FLUENCY How do Little Gorilla's friends and family show they love him? (Possible responses: They hold him; kiss him; play with him; help him; watch over him; they give him a birthday party.)

BIRTHDAY PARTY INVITATIONS

All Levels Have children work with partners. Invite each pair to make an invitation to Little Gorilla's birthday party. Suggest that they tell who the party is for and when and where the party will be held. Encourage them to decorate their invitations with animals or forest plants. Display the invitations on a bulletin board in the classroom. WRITING

TALK TO THE ANIMALS

Early Production/Speech Emergence/ Intermediate Fluency Invite children to pretend that they are Little Gorilla. Encourage them to look through the story to find the pictures of other animals. Review with children what happens on those pages. Have them tell what Little Gorilla might say to each animal he sees in the big green forest. LISTENING/SPEAKING

WRITING STORIES

Speech Emergence/Intermediate Fluency Invite children to write a story about Little Gorilla. Suggest that they write a story to tell what happens to Little Gorilla after his birthday party. Encourage them to draw pictures to show what happens at the beginning, in the middle, and at the end of the story. Then ask volunteers to show their pictures and read their stories aloud. LISTENING/READING/WRITING

TRADE BOOK

Brown Bear, Brown Bear, What Do You See? by Bill Martin, Jr. Holt, Inc., 1967. Children will learn the names of animals and colors.

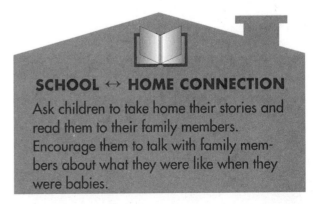

SCHOOL ↔ HOME CONNECTION Ask children to take home their stories and read them to their family members. Encourage them to talk with family members about what they were like when they were babies.

Any Kind of Dog

BUILDING BACKGROUND

Prior Knowledge

Talk with children about young animals. Ask volunteers to name baby animals, such as puppy, kitten, chick, lamb, and cub. Ask what each animal is called when it grows up. Encourage children to talk about animals that live in their native countries.

TPR: Total Physical Response

Read aloud the following rhyme, and demonstrate the actions. Then have children follow the motions as you read the rhyme again.

> *Call the puppy and give it some milk.*
> *Brush his coat 'til it shines like silk.*
> *Call the dog and give him a bone.*
> *Take him for a walk, and then put him in*
> *his home.*

Develop Oral Language

Display the following rhyme, and read it aloud, emphasizing the names of the animals as you read. Then have children repeat the rhyme with you several times. You may wish to point to the following illustrations in "Any Kind of Dog": lamb, bear, mouse, caterpillar, alligator, dog, pony.

A lamb becomes a sheep.
A cub becomes a bear.
A pony becomes a galloping horse,
Running everywhere.
A tiny mouse grows big and fat.
A caterpillar changes.
An alligator gets long and strong,
With jaws like steel cages!
But a puppy makes a very nice pet,
Wagging its tail from top to end,
And best of all a puppy becomes —
A dog that's your best friend.

BUILDING CONCEPTS

Use Poster 11: "Baby Animals"

Poster 11 shows young animals and their adult counterparts. Point to each pair of animals, and have volunteers name them. Invite children to tell which animals are wild, which are farm animals, and which would make good pets. Use Poster 11 to help children continue their discussion of animals.

Write these concept words from "Any Kind of Dog" on the board. Read them aloud and describe the sound each animal makes or its size: *dog, caterpillar, mouse, alligator, lamb, pony, bear.*

Rereading

Invite children to reread the rhyme with you. Have them point to any concept words they see illustrated on Poster 11.

Speech Emergence Invite children to pretend they have a new puppy. Ask what they will name the puppy. Have them tell why.

Copying Master

Use page 43 to help make the concepts more comprehensible.

TIPS FOR CLASSROOM MANAGEMENT

You may want to have children read a translation of "Any Kind of Dog" in their first language with family members. See *Anthology Translation Booklets.*

Harcourt Brace School Publishers

Any Kind of Dog

A. Who is in the pet shop? Talk about the animals with a partner. Label the animals.

dog	caterpillar	mouse	alligator	lamb	pony	bear

B. Share this page with your family.

TIPS FOR CLASSROOM MANAGEMENT To prepare children to read "Any Kind of Dog," use page 44 to provide additional concepts and language.

BEFORE READING PAGES 10–21

Read aloud the title, and look at the illustrations on pages 10–21 with children. Then display pages 12–17, and say

- This boy wanted a dog.
- His mother said a dog was too much trouble.
- His mother gave him a caterpillar.
- The caterpillar was nice.
- It looked a little like a dog.
- But it was not a dog.
- His mother gave him a mouse.
- The mouse was nice.
- It looked a little like a dog.
- But it was not a dog.

Display pages 18–21, and say

- His mother gave him a baby alligator.
- The baby alligator was nice.
- It looked a little like a dog.
- But it was not a dog.
- His mother gave him a lamb.
- The lamb was nice.
- It looked a little like a dog.
- But it was not a dog.

Then ask children these questions:

PREPRODUCTION/EARLY PRODUCTION

- Is this story about a girl? (no)
- Did the boy want a cat or a dog? (dog)

SPEECH EMERGENCE/INTERMEDIATE FLUENCY

- What animals did the boy's mother give him? (caterpillar, mouse, baby alligator, lamb)
- Why didn't the mother want a dog? (A dog was too much trouble.)

BEFORE READING PAGES 22–32

Look at the illustrations on pages 22–32 with children. Then display pages 22–27, and say

- His mother gave him a pony.
- The pony was nice.
- It looked a little like a dog.
- But it was not a dog.
- His mother gave him a lion.
- The lion was nice.
- It looked a little like a dog.
- But it was not a dog.
- His mother gave him a bear.
- The bear was nice.
- It looked a little like a dog.
- But it was not a dog.

Display pages 28–32, and say

- All of the animals were nice.
- But the boy wanted a dog.
- His mother gave him a dog.
- The dog was nice.
- It looked just like a dog.
- The dog was a lot of trouble.
- But the boy loved the dog.

Then ask children these questions:

PREPRODUCTION/EARLY PRODUCTION

- Did the mother give the boy a tiger? (no)
- Did the boy get a dog at the end of the story? (yes)

SPEECH EMERGENCE/INTERMEDIATE FLUENCY

- Why do you think the mother gave the boy a dog? (Possible response: She wanted to make him happy.)
- What was the boy's new dog like? (Possible responses: It was nice; it looked just like a dog; it was a lot of trouble.)

READING THE LITERATURE Have children join the Strategic Reading group and do a shared reading with English-fluent partners.

Harcourt Brace School Publishers

Responding to the Literature

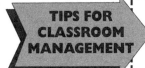

TIPS FOR CLASSROOM MANAGEMENT

IF children need additional support, **THEN** complete the Comprehension Check using appropriately leveled questions. You may also have them participate in the My Favorite Dog activity.

COMPREHENSION CHECK

All Levels These questions can serve as models to meet the needs of the various language levels of your children.

PREPRODUCTION Did the boy want one special kind of dog? (no)

EARLY PRODUCTION Did the boy already have pet fish or a pet cat? (pet fish) Instead of a dog, did the boy's mother give him real animals or stuffed animals? (stuffed animals)

SPEECH EMERGENCE Why do you think the other animals were not too much trouble? (Possible response: They weren't real.)

INTERMEDIATE FLUENCY How can a dog be a lot of trouble? (Possible responses: A dog needs to be walked; a dog needs to be fed and cared for; a dog needs lots of love and attention.)

HOW TO CARE FOR A DOG

All Levels Have children work in small groups to brainstorm a list of things that dog owners must do to care for their pets. Encourage children to write their ideas on paper or dictate them to you. Invite groups to share their ideas with each other. LISTENING/SPEAKING/WRITING

How to Care for a Dog

Give it food.   Give it water.
Walk it.   Brush it.
Play with it.

MY FAVORITE DOG

Early Production/Speech Emergence Ask children to draw a picture of a dog that they would like to have. Then invite volunteers to share their pictures and describe their dogs. Encourage classmates to ask questions about the dogs in the pictures. LISTENING/SPEAKING

WRITING A STORY

Speech Emergence/Intermediate Fluency Invite children to write stories about a girl who wants a cat. Have them tell about animals that the girl's mother gives her instead of a cat. Children can use the Big Book as a model. Encourage them to draw pictures to show what happens in their stories. Ask volunteers to share their stories. LISTENING/SPEAKING/WRITING

ESL/TITLE I LIBRARY

I Want a Pet by Barbara Gregorich. School Zone, 1992. A boy searches for a particular pet. **Available on ESL/Title I Audiocassette.**

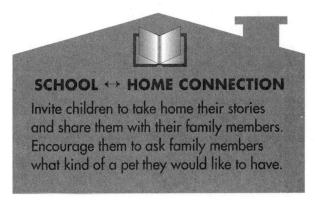

SCHOOL ↔ HOME CONNECTION

Invite children to take home their stories and share them with their family members. Encourage them to ask family members what kind of a pet they would like to have.

Harcourt Brace School Publishers

Introducing the Literature

The Lion and the Mouse

BUILDING BACKGROUND

Prior Knowledge

Discuss opposites with children. Invite volunteers to brainstorm a list of opposites such as *no, yes; can, can't; big, small; happy, sad; day, night;* and *fat, thin.* Record opposite word pairs on poster board, and then display the list.

TPR: Total Physical Response

To develop this concept further, say the word *big* as you stretch up tall, and then say the word *small* as you crouch down. Demonstrate other opposite pairs, such as *smile/frown* and *up/down.* Invite children to imitate your actions and, if possible, suggest others of their own.

Develop Oral Language

Display the following rhyme. Read it aloud, emphasizing the beat. Invite children to read the rhyme with you as you repeat it several times. Use the pictures of the lion and the mouse in "The Lion and the Mouse" to help children visualize *big* and *little.* Use your hands to demonstrate *up* and *down.*

> Said the Lion to the Mouse —
> I say, "Stop!"
> You say, "Go!"
> I say, "Yes!"
> You say, "No!"
> You run up,
> Then run down.
> I have a big smile.
> You have a little frown.
> We're not alike.
> We're different as can be.
> But I like you,
> And you like me!
> On that —
> The Lion and the Mouse agree!

BUILDING CONCEPTS

Use Poster 12: "Opposites"

Poster 12 gives children the opportunity to identify opposites. Invite them to look at the pictures of the mouse and the lion. Have volunteers describe the balls and the kites that the friends have. Ask them about the signs the animals are holding. Use Poster 12 to help children continue to talk about opposites.

Write these concept words from "The Lion and the Mouse" on the board: *up, down, stop, go, yes, no, big, little.* Read each one aloud. Use pantomime to illustrate their meanings.

Rereading

Invite children to reread the rhyme with you. Have them point to any illustrated concept words pictured on Poster 12.

Intermediate Fluency Ask children to find other examples of opposite word pairs to add to the group-generated list.

Copying Master

Use page 47 to help make the concepts more comprehensible.

TIPS FOR CLASSROOM MANAGEMENT

You may want to have children read a translation of "The Lion and the Mouse" in their first language with family members. See *Anthology Translation Booklets.*

Harcourt Brace School Publishers

The Lion and the Mouse

A. Work with a partner. Tell about each picture. Use a word in the box. Write the word under the picture.

no	down	go	little

up _____

stop _____

big _____

yes _____

B. Share this page with your family.

Harcourt Brace School Publishers

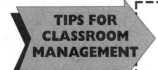

To prepare children to read "The Lion and the Mouse," use page 48 to provide additional concepts and language.

BEFORE READING PAGES 36–46

Share the title with children, and then invite them to look at the illustrations on pages 36–46. Display pages 38–40 for all to see, and say

- This is a little mouse. This is his house.
- The mouse ran out of his house.
- He wanted to have fun.
- This is a big lion.
- The lion was sleeping.
- The mouse ran up and down the lion.
- The lion was mad.
- The lion said he would eat the mouse.

Display pages 41–46 for all to see. Use a high, squeaky tone for the mouse's voice and a loud, low tone for the lion's voice. Say

- The mouse said, "Let me go!"
- The lion said, "No!"
- The mouse said he would help the lion.
- The lion said the mouse was too little.
- The mouse said, "I can help you."
- The lion liked the mouse.
- The lion let the mouse go.
- The mouse ran away.

Then ask children these questions:

PREPRODUCTION/EARLY PRODUCTION

- Is this story about a mouse? (yes)
- Is this story about a lion? (yes)
- Did the lion want to eat the mouse or play with him? (eat him)

SPEECH EMERGENCE/INTERMEDIATE FLUENCY

- How did the mouse stop the lion from eating him? (The mouse said he would help the lion.)
- Why did the lion let the mouse go? (He liked the mouse.)

BEFORE READING PAGES 47–50

Look at the illustrations on pages 47–50 with children. Display pages 47–48 for all to see, point to the appropriate pictures, and say

- The mouse ran out of his house again.
- The lion was in a net.
- The lion could not get out.
- "Help! Help!" roared the lion.
- The mouse nibbled at the net.
- He nibbled and nibbled.

Pantomime the mouse nibbling at the net. Then display pages 49–50 for all to see, point to the appropriate pictures, and say

- The net came down.
- The lion came out.
- The lion was happy.
- The mouse had helped the lion.
- The lion and the mouse were friends.
- The mouse was small, but he could do big things, too.

Then ask children these questions:

PREPRODUCTION/EARLY PRODUCTION

- Was the lion in a cage? (no)
- Was the lion in a net? (yes)
- Who helped the lion, the mouse or another lion? (the mouse)

SPEECH EMERGENCE/INTERMEDIATE FLUENCY

- Who came to help the lion? (the mouse)
- What happened at the end of the story? (Possible response: The mouse helped the lion get out of the net.)
- What does this story tell you about being small? (Possible response: Even if you are small, you can do big things.)

READING THE LITERATURE Have children join the Strategic Reading group and read the selection with English-fluent partners.

Harcourt Brace School Publishers

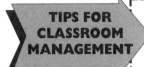

Responding to the Literature

TIPS FOR CLASSROOM MANAGEMENT

IF children need additional support, **THEN** complete Working with "The Lion and the Mouse" on page T85 in the *Warm Friends* Teacher's Edition.

COMPREHENSION CHECK

All Levels These questions can serve as models to meet the needs of the various language levels of your children.

PREPRODUCTION Did the mouse and the lion become friends in this story? (yes)

EARLY PRODUCTION Who was big, the mouse or the lion? (the lion)

SPEECH EMERGENCE Why did the mouse climb on the lion? (Possible response: The mouse was playing.) Where did the mouse live? (in a tree)

INTERMEDIATE FLUENCY How did the mouse help the lion? (He helped him get out of the net by nibbling on it.)

OPPOSITES BOOK

All Levels Invite children to make pages for an Opposites Book. Review the list of opposite word pairs generated during Prior Knowledge. Have children brainstorm additional word pairs to add to the list. Invite children to work with partners to select a word pair and draw pictures to illustrate the words. If possible, children can write labels or sentences to go with their pictures. Combine the completed pages to form an Opposites Book. LISTENING/ SPEAKING/WRITING

ACT OUT THE STORY

Early Production/Speech Emergence Invite pairs of children to act out the first part of the story, in which the lion catches the mouse and says he is going to eat him. Then have them act out the end of the story, in which the mouse helps the lion. LISTENING/SPEAKING

WRITING STORIES

Speech Emergence/Intermediate Fluency Have children write their own stories about the lion and the mouse. Suggest that they write a story about what the two friends do together after the lion gets out of the net. Encourage them to write about another way in which the lion and the mouse help each other. Invite them to read their stories aloud. READING/WRITING

ESL/TITLE I LIBRARY

Too Much by Dorothy Stott. Puffin Unicorn Books, 1990. Little Duck runs into trouble as he searches for a place to swim. **Available on ESL/Title I Audiocassette.**

SCHOOL ↔ HOME CONNECTION
Invite children to take home their stories and read them to family members. Ask them to talk with family members about times they have helped other people.

Harcourt Brace School Publishers

Introducing the Literature

My Best Friend

BUILDING BACKGROUND

Prior Knowledge
Talk with children about their best friends. Encourage volunteers to name things that their best friends can do well. Then have them name things that they can do that their best friends cannot.

TPR: Total Physical Response
Read aloud the following rhyme, and demonstrate the actions. Then read it again, and have children follow the actions in the rhyme.

> Find a friend and hop, hop, hop.
> When we're tired, we stop, stop, stop.
> We turn around, and count to ten.
> Find another friend and do it again!

Develop Oral Language
Display the following rhyme. Read it aloud, emphasizing the rhyming words. Then invite children to read the rhyme with you several times. You may want to use illustrations in "My Best Friend" to help children visualize the following: friend, eat, spaghetti, table, clean, paint, paper, run, jump, climb, tree, read, book.

> My friend can eat spaghetti,
>   And keep the table clean.
> My friend can paint on paper,
>   And her hands don't turn all green.
>
> My friend can run and jump,
>   And climb up in a tree.
> My friend can read a book.
>   She reads aloud to me!
>
> It's fun to have a friend
>   Who's smart and funny, too.
> And who likes me as a friend
>   Because of what I do.

BUILDING CONCEPTS

POSTER

Poster 13: "Friends Together"
Poster 13 shows things that two friends can do together. Point to the pictures in turn and have children tell what the friends like to do together. (eat spaghetti, paint, climb, run, read) Use Poster 13 to help children talk about things that they like to do with their own friends.

Write these concept words from "My Best Friend" on the board. Read them aloud as you point to each one: *run, climb, jump, eat, paint, read.* Use pantomime to help children understand the words.

Rereading
Invite children to reread the rhyme with you. Have them point to any concept words pictured on Poster 13.

MEETING INDIVIDUAL NEEDS

Extra Support Have children draw a picture of themselves doing something with their best friend.

Copying Master
Use page 51 to help make the concepts more comprehensible.

TIPS FOR CLASSROOM MANAGEMENT

You may want to have children read a translation of "My Best Friend" in their first language with family members. See *Anthology Translation Booklets.*

Harcourt Brace School Publishers

NAME _____

My Best Friend

run   eat

jump   paint

climb   read

A. Talk about the pictures. Write a word that tells about each one.

_____

- -

_____

_____

- -

_____

_____

- -

_____

B. Share this page with your family.

TIPS FOR CLASSROOM MANAGEMENT

To prepare children to read "My Best Friend," use page 52 to provide additional concepts and language.

BEFORE READING PAGES 58–66

Read aloud the title of the book, and invite children to look at the illustrations on pages 58–66 with you. Hold up pages 60–64 for all to see, point to the appropriate pictures, and say

- This is a girl. This is her best friend.
- The girl's best friend is coming over.
- The girls will spend the night together.
- The girl's best friend can run faster than anyone.
- She can climb higher than anyone.
- She can jump farther than anyone.
- The girl is glad to have her as a best friend.

Demonstrate each of the actions: running, climbing, and jumping. Then display pages 65–66 for all to see, point to the appropriate pictures, and say

- The girl eats spaghetti with a fork.
- She drops spaghetti on the table.
- The girl's best friend doesn't drop any on the table.
- The girl paints pictures.
- She makes a mess.
- The girl's best friend paints pictures.
- She does not make a mess.

Then ask children these questions:

PREPRODUCTION/EARLY PRODUCTION

- Is this story about two best friends? (yes)
- Do the friends run, climb, and jump? (yes)

SPEECH EMERGENCE/INTERMEDIATE FLUENCY

- How does the girl feel about her best friend? (Possible response: The girl is glad she is her best friend.)
- What do the girl and her best friend do together? (They run, climb, and jump; they eat spaghetti; they paint pictures.)

BEFORE READING PAGES 67–74

Look at the illustrations on pages 67–74 with children. Hold up pages 67–69 for all to see, point to the appropriate pictures, and say

- The girl's best friend can untie her shoelaces.
- She can do up her buttons.
- She knows how to read.
- The girl is glad to have her as a best friend.

Pantomime the actions. Then display pages 70–74 for all to see, point to appropriate pictures, and say

- The girl's best friend is scared.
- She thinks there's a monster in the room.
- The girl knows there is no monster.
- The girl knows that it is the wind.
- The wind is blowing the curtains.
- The girl closes the window.
- Now the curtains won't blow.
- The girl's best friend is happy.
- She is glad to have a best friend, too.

Then ask children these questions:

PREPRODUCTION/EARLY PRODUCTION

- Can the girl's best friend untie her shoelaces? (yes)
- Who gets scared of a monster, the girl or her best friend? (her best friend)
- Who closes the window, the girl or her best friend? (the girl)

SPEECH EMERGENCE/INTERMEDIATE FLUENCY

- Who is glad to have a best friend? (both girls)
- How does the girl help her best friend? (Possible response: She closes the window so the curtains won't blow.)

READING THE LITERATURE Have children join the Strategic Reading group and read the selection with English-fluent partners.

Harcourt Brace School Publishers

Responding to the Literature

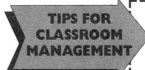

TIPS FOR CLASSROOM MANAGEMENT

IF children need additional support, **THEN** complete Working with "My Best Friend" on page T137 in the *Warm Friends* Teacher's Edition.

COMPREHENSION CHECK

All Levels These questions can serve as models to meet the needs of the various language levels of your children.

PREPRODUCTION Do the two girls like being best friends? (yes)

EARLY PRODUCTION Do the girls have a sleepover or do they just spend the day together? (have a sleepover)

SPEECH EMERGENCE Who else do you see in this story besides the girl and her best friend? (the girls' mothers) Where are the two girls when they run, climb, and jump? (outside)

INTERMEDIATE FLUENCY How does the girl help her best friend? (Possible response: She closes the window. She shows her that there is no monster in the room.) Why is it nice to have a best friend? (Responses will vary.)

FRIENDSHIP WEB

All Levels Invite small groups of children to work together to make a friendship web. Have them write the word *Friend* in the center of the web. Then have them brainstorm words that describe a friend. Ask them to write those words around the word *Friend*. Display the webs, and encourage the groups to compare their work. LISTENING/SPEAKING/WRITING

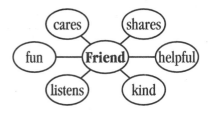

THINGS I CAN DO WELL

Early Production/Speech Emergence/ Intermediate Fluency Remind children that even though some of our friends can do things better than we can, everyone is good at something. Invite partners to brainstorm things they like to do and can do well. Then ask each partner to make his or her own list. Some children may want to use drawings to record their ideas. Encourage partners to compare their lists. LISTENING/SPEAKING/WRITING

WRITING STORIES

Speech Emergence/Intermediate Fluency Invite children to write stories about their best friends. Suggest that they tell what that friend can do better than they can do and whether this is important to know. Have them also tell what they can do better than their friend. Encourage children to illustrate their writing. Ask volunteers to share their pictures and read their stories. READING/WRITING

TRADE BOOK
Yo! Yes? by Chris Raschka. Orchard, 1993. Two boys meet on the street and become friends.

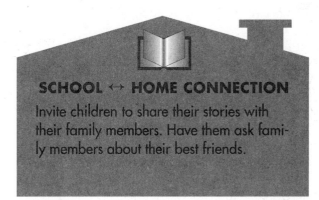

SCHOOL ↔ HOME CONNECTION
Invite children to share their stories with their family members. Have them ask family members about their best friends.

Harcourt Brace School Publishers

BUILDING BACKGROUND

Prior Knowledge

Discuss animal sounds with children. Have volunteers name animals and the sounds they make. You may wish to begin with an example such as *A cat says meow*. Encourage children to identify animals that they have heard here or in other countries.

TPR: Total Physical Response

To develop this concept further, display pictures of animals, such as a cow, a cat, a dog, and a bee. Point to each picture and imitate the sound that the animal in the picture makes. Then select a picture and invite volunteers to make the animal's sound.

Develop Oral Language

Display the following rhyme. Read it aloud, emphasizing the sound words. Then invite children to read the rhyme with you several times. You may want to point to the following pictures in "Splash, Splash": bee, water, cow, pig, cake, cat, lake, frog.

A bee fell in the water,
    Then quickly flew away—buzz, buzz!
A cow fell in the water,
    And then ran the other way—moo, moo!
A pig fell in the water,
    As he dreamed of eating cake—oink, oink!
A cat fell in the water,
    Then jumped out of the lake—meow, meow!
A frog fell in the water,
    And flapped his froggy feet.
He said swimming in the water
    Is oh, so very sweet—ribbit, ribbit!

BUILDING CONCEPTS

 Use Poster 14: "Animal Sounds"
Poster 14 provides children with the opportunity to identify animal sounds. Have children point to specific animals as you name them. Then ask volunteers to name the sound that each animal makes. Ask volunteers to tell which animals enjoy being in the lake. (frog, duck) Ask which animals would rather be on dry land. (bee, pig, cow, cat)

Write these concept words from "Splash, Splash" on the board: *bee, pig, cow, cat, frog*. Help children write each word on a flash card. When you reread the rhyme, they can hold up each flash card at the appropriate time.

Rereading

Invite children to reread the rhyme with you. Have them point to pictures on Poster 14 that illustrate the concept words.

 Challenge Ask children to name animals that make loud sounds and animals that make soft sounds.

MEETING INDIVIDUAL NEEDS

Copying Master

Use page 55 to help make the concepts more comprehensible.

TIPS FOR CLASSROOM MANAGEMENT

You may want to have children read "Splash, Splash" in their first language with family members. See *Anthology Translation Booklets*.

Harcourt Brace School Publishers

Splash, Splash

A. Work with a partner. Talk about the animals. Read the clues. Write the animal names.

frog

cat

cow

pig

bee

❶ I say, "Buzz." _____
_____

❷ I say, "Ribbit." _____
_____

❸ I say, "Meow." _____
_____

❹ I say, "Moo." _____
_____

❺ I say, "Oink." _____

B. Share this page with your family.

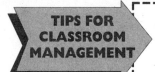
To prepare children to read "Splash, Splash," use page 56 to provide additional concepts and language.

BEFORE READING PAGES 80–97

Read aloud the title. Then look at the illustrations on pages 80–97 with children. Display pages 82–89, and say

- This is a bee. The bee fell in the water.
- The bee says, "Buzz, splash, buzz."
- This is a mouse.
- The mouse fell in the water.
- He got water in his ears.
- He got water in his eyes.
- The mouse says, "Squeak, splash, squeak."
- This is a pig. The pig fell in the water.
- The pig says, "Oink, splash, oink."

Display pages 90–97, and say

- This is a dog. The dog fell in the water.
- He liked it.
- He went in again.
- The dog says, "Ruff, splash, ruff."
- This is a cow. The cow fell in the water.
- She looked unhappy.
- Cows don't like to swim.
- The cow says, "Moo, splash, moo."

Then ask children these questions:

PREPRODUCTION/EARLY PRODUCTION

- Did the animals fall in the grass? (no)
- Which animal says, "Buzz, splash, buzz," the bee or the dog? (the bee)

SPEECH EMERGENCE/INTERMEDIATE FLUENCY

- Which animal went into the water again? (the dog)
- What happened to the mouse in this story? (He fell in the water. He got water in his ears and eyes.)
- What happened to the pig in this story? (He fell in the water.)

BEFORE READING PAGES 98–112

Look at the illustrations on pages 98–112 with children. Then display pages 98–105, and say

- This is a duck.
- The duck fell in the water.
- Ducks know about water.
- They paddle on the water.
- The duck says, "Quack, splash, quack."
- This is a cat.
- The cat fell in the water.
- The cat was not happy.
- Cats look small when they fall into the water.
- The cat says "Meow, splash, meow."

Display pages 106–112, and say

- This is a frog.
- The frog fell in the water.
- The frog likes to splash in the water.
- The frog says, "Ribbit, splash, ribbit."
- Now all the animals are in the water.
- They are playing.

Then ask children these questions:

PREPRODUCTION/EARLY PRODUCTION

- Did a duck fall in the water? (yes)
- Did a horse fall in the water? (no)
- Who likes the water, the duck or the cat? (the duck)

SPEECH EMERGENCE/INTERMEDIATE FLUENCY

- What made the splash sound in this story? (The animals falling into the water.)
- Look at all the animals again. What sound does each one make? (Possible responses: buzz, squeak, oink, ruff, moo, quack, meow, ribbit)

Harcourt Brace School Publishers

READING THE LITERATURE Have children join the Strategic Reading group and do a shared reading of the selection with English-fluent partners.

Responding to the Literature

TIPS FOR CLASSROOM MANAGEMENT

IF children need additional support, **THEN** complete the Comprehension Check using appropriately leveled questions. You may also want to have them participate in the Old MacDonald activity.

COMPREHENSION CHECK

All Levels These questions can serve as models to meet the needs of the various language levels of your children.

PREPRODUCTION Is this story about the sounds that people make? (no) Is this story about the sounds that animals make? (yes)

EARLY PRODUCTION Did the animals fall in the ocean or in a lake? (a lake) Were the animals having fun in the water at the end of the story or were they afraid of the water? (having fun)

SPEECH EMERGENCE Which animals in the story have wings? (bee and duck) Which animal in the story has flappy feet? (frog)

INTERMEDIATE FLUENCY What were the animals doing at the end of the story? (Possible responses: diving, swimming, wading, and playing in the water) Which animal do you think likes the water best? Why? (Responses will vary.)

ANIMAL SOUNDS CHART

All Levels Make a group chart showing the animals and sounds in "Splash, Splash." Ask children how the sounds are different in their first language. Then have them brainstorm names of other animals and the sounds they make. Record their ideas. LISTENING/SPEAKING

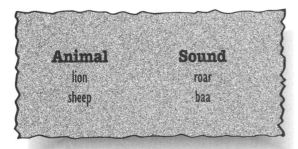

Animal	Sound
lion	roar
sheep	baa

OLD MACDONALD

Speech Emergence/Intermediate Fluency
With children, sing "Old MacDonald." Then sing a version that includes all the animals from the story. Model the first verse of the song. LISTENING/SPEAKING

Old MacDonald had a farm, E-I-E-I-O.
And on the farm he had a bee, E-I-E-I-O.
With a buzz, buzz here,
And a buzz, buzz there.
Here a buzz, there a buzz,
Everywhere a buzz, buzz.
Old MacDonald had a farm, E-I-E-I-O.

WRITING STORIES

Speech Emergence/Intermediate Fluency
Ask children to write a scene about another animal that fell into the water. Encourage children to include animal sounds in their stories. WRITING

ESL/TITLE I LIBRARY
Look What I Can Do by Jose Aruego. Aladdin Books, 1971. Two water buffalo try to outdo each other. **Available on ESL/Title I Audiocassette.**

SCHOOL ↔ HOME CONNECTION
Have children take home their story scenes and read them to their family members. Ask them to report back on what their family members thought.

Introducing the Literature

BUILDING BACKGROUND

Prior Knowledge
Talk with children about frogs. Have volunteers describe a frog. Talk with them about how frogs move. You may wish to have children say the word *frog* in their native language.

TPR: Total Physical Response
To further develop the concept of ways to move, invite children to move like frogs. Guide them to crouch like frogs and then jump up. Suggest that they hop and leap around the room. Direct children to make frog sounds as they move. You may also want to take students outside and show them how to play Leap Frog.

Develop Oral Language
Display the following rhyme, and read it aloud. Then invite children to reread the rhyme with you several times. You may want to drop leaves to help children visualize the word *float*.

> I am a little frog,
> But hopping is not for me.
> I like to watch as leaves float down
> And blow beneath the trees.
>
> Leaping, turning, twisting —
> Now, I'm moving in the breeze.
> Instead of hopping, I'm dancing,
> As pretty as you please!

BUILDING CONCEPTS

Poster 15: "Frogs"
Poster 15 shows frogs near a pond. Ask volunteers to look at the frogs and tell what they are doing. Ask how these frogs are the same as real frogs. Then talk with children about how these frogs are different from real frogs. Help children recognize that real frogs do not dance, wear sunglasses, or act like people.

Write these concept words from "Hop Jump" on the board: *float, leaping, turning, twisting, dancing, hopping*. Read them aloud as you point to each one. Act out each word to help children understand its meaning.

Rereading
Invite children to read the rhyme with you again. Have them point to any concept words pictured on Poster 15.

MEETING INDIVIDUAL NEEDS

Speech Emergence Ask volunteers to name things that float in the air or on the water.

Copying Master
Use page 59 to help make the concepts more comprehensible.

TIPS FOR CLASSROOM MANAGEMENT

You may want to have children read a translation of "Hop Jump" in their first language with family members. See *Anthology Translation Booklets*.

Harcourt Brace School Publishers

Hop Jump

A. Work with a partner. Talk about the pictures. Try to decide which sentence goes with each picture.

The frog is **leaping** to the other lily pad.

The frog is **turning** the other way.

The frog is **hopping** near the pond.

The frog is **twisting** his body.

The frog is **dancing** with a friend.

The frogs like to **float** in the water.

B. Share this page with your family.

To prepare children to read "Hop Jump," use page 60 to provide additional concepts and language.

BEFORE READING PAGES 116–125

Share the title and look through the illustrations on pages 116–125 with children. Then hold up pages 116–121 for all to see, and say

- These are frogs.
- This frog is Betsy.
- Betsy watches the other frogs.
- The frogs hop jump, hop jump.
- The frogs always do the same thing.

Hold up pages 122–125, and say

- Betsy watches some leaves float down.
- The leaves are leaping, turning, twisting.
- The leaves do different things.
- Betsy tries to move like the leaves.
- She cannot float in the air.
- But she can do other things.
- Betsy starts leaping, turning, and twisting.
- Betsy calls it dancing.

Then ask children these questions:

PREPRODUCTION/EARLY PRODUCTION

- Is this story about frogs? (yes)
- Is one frog named Betsy? (yes)
- Does Betsy watch other frogs or fish? (other frogs)
- Does Betsy hop and jump or does she dance? (dance)

SPEECH EMERGENCE/INTERMEDIATE FLUENCY

- What does Betsy watch right before she starts dancing? (leaves)
- How is Betsy moving when she dances? (leaping, turning, and twisting)
- How are the leaves that Betsy watches different from the frogs that she watches? (The leaves do different things. The frogs always do the same thing.)

BEFORE READING PAGES 126–140

Look at the illustrations on pages 126–140 with children. Then hold up pages 126–131 for all to see, point to the appropriate pictures, and say

- The other frogs come back.
- They hop jump, hop jump.
- There is no room for Betsy to dance.
- Betsy goes to find a place for dancing.

Hold up pages 132–140 for all to see, point to the appropriate pictures, and say

- The other frogs want to know about dancing.
- They go to see Betsy.
- They move their feet.
- They start dancing, too.
- One frog is still hopping.
- Betsy says there is room for dancing and hopping.

Then ask children these questions:

PREPRODUCTION/EARLY PRODUCTION

- Does Betsy find a place to dance? (yes)
- Do the other frogs go to see Betsy dance? (yes)
- Do all of the other frogs dance with Betsy? (no)

SPEECH EMERGENCE/INTERMEDIATE FLUENCY

- Why do the other frogs go to look for Betsy? (Possible response: They want to know how to dance.)
- What does Betsy say at the end of the story? (that there is room for dancing and hopping)
- Why do you think Betsy started dancing? (Possible response: She was tired of hopping and jumping.)

READING THE LITERATURE Have children join the Strategic Reading group and read the selection with English-fluent partners.

Responding to the Literature

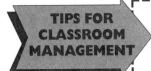

TIPS FOR CLASSROOM MANAGEMENT

IF children need additional support, **THEN** complete Working with "Hop Jump" on page T233 in the *Warm Friends* Teacher's Edition.

COMPREHENSION CHECK

All Levels These questions can serve as models to meet the needs of the various language levels of your children.

PREPRODUCTION Do the frogs in this story look like real frogs? (yes)

EARLY PRODUCTION Do real frogs dance or do they hop and jump? (hop and jump)

SPEECH EMERGENCE What do the other frogs do at the beginning of the story? (hop, jump) What does Betsy do that the other frogs do not do at first? (dance)

INTERMEDIATE FLUENCY Do you think Betsy is happy that the other frogs joined her? Why or why not? (Possible response: Yes; it is more fun to dance with others.)

LISTING WORDS

All Levels Have children work in small groups. Work with children to brainstorm a list of words that describe what they do when they dance. Help them record their suggestions. Ask groups to share their lists with each other by reading them aloud and acting out the moves. LISTENING/SPEAKING/READING/WRITING

When we dance, we . . .
twist.   move our heads.
turn.   bend our knees.
swing our arms.   hop and jump.

DANCE MOVEMENTS

Early Production/Speech Emergence Play some gentle music for children and invite them to pretend they are Betsy. Encourage them to dance to the music. Give them commands as they dance, such as, *Start twisting. Now start turning like leaves. Now start leaping.* Then have children improvise dance movements of their own. After the dancing, ask children to describe the ways that they moved to the music. LISTENING/SPEAKING

WRITING STORIES

Speech Emergence/Intermediate Fluency Ask children to write stories about another frog in Betsy's pond that does something different, such as sing songs instead of dance or hop. Children can use "Hop Jump" as a model and draw pictures to illustrate their words. Invite them to display the pictures and read the stories aloud. READING/WRITING

TRADE BOOK

Slither, Swoop, Swing by Alex Ayliffe. Viking, 1992. The animals of the world move in many different ways.

SCHOOL ↔ HOME CONNECTION
Invite children to take home their stories. Have them ask family members to tell about a time when they did something different.

Harcourt Brace School Publishers

Introducing the Literature

EEK! There's a Mouse in the House

BUILDING BACKGROUND

Prior Knowledge

Remind children that rhyming words are words that end with the same sound, such as *cat* and *fat*. Then invite volunteers to name rhyming word pairs.

TPR: Total Physical Response

To develop this concept further, tell children that you will read aloud some words. Ask them to stand up whenever they hear two words that rhyme. Then read aloud word pairs such as the following: *mouse/house, dog/cat, table/chair, cake/lake, cow/now, sheep/lamb, door/more, hen/chicken, wall/all.*

Develop Oral Language

Display the following rhyme. Read it aloud, emphasizing the rhyming words. Then invite children to reread the rhyme with you several times. You may want to point to the following illustrations in "EEK! There's a Mouse in the House": mouse, cat, dish, fish, hog, dog, sheep, yarn, mop.

> What's bigger than a mouse? A rat!
> Who chases a rat? A cat!
> What's flat like a plate? A dish!
> What's served on a dish? A fish!
> What's bigger than a pig? A hog!
> What's not like a hog? A dog!
> What's made from sheep's wool? Soft yarn!
> Where does a sheep sleep? In the barn!
> What cleans like a broom? A mop!
> Who uses a mop? My pop!

BUILDING CONCEPTS

POSTER

Use Poster 16: "Rhyming Words"

Poster 16 provides an opportunity for children to identify rhyming words. Ask volunteers to name the animals on the poster. Ask children to point to the mop. Then have a volunteer name a rhyming word that is pictured. (stop) Have children find other pairs of rhyming words pictured on Poster 16. (Possible responses: cat/rat; fish/dish; hog/dog; yarn/barn; house/mouse)

Write these concept words from "EEK! There's a Mouse in the House" on the board: *house, rat, dish, fish, hog, mop, yarn, barn.* Use pictures to illustrate the meanings of unfamiliar words.

Rereading

Invite children to read the rhyme with you again. Have them point to illustrations of concept words on Poster 16.

MEETING INDIVIDUAL NEEDS

Speech Emergence Help children to name as many words as possible that rhyme with *cat*.

Copying Master

Use page 63 to help make the concepts more comprehensible.

TIPS FOR CLASSROOM MANAGEMENT

You may want to have children read a translation of "EEK! There's a Mouse in the House" in their first language with family members. See *Anthology Translation Booklets*.

Harcourt Brace School Publishers

EEK! There's a Mouse in the House

A. Work with a partner. Name the pictures. Name words in the box that rhyme with each picture. Write the words.

rat	hog	mop	dish	house	barn

stop _____

mouse _____

dog _____

cat _____

fish _____

yarn _____

B. Share this page with your family.

TIPS FOR CLASSROOM MANAGEMENT

To prepare children to read "EEK! There's a Mouse in the House," use page 64 to provide additional concepts and language.

BEFORE READING PAGES 146–154

Read aloud the title and invite children to join you in looking at the illustrations on pages 146–154. Then hold up pages 148–151 for all to see, point to the appropriate pictures, and say

- There's a mouse in the house!
- The cat comes in to chase the mouse.
- The cat knocks over a lamp.
- The dog comes in to catch the cat.
- The dog breaks a dish.
- The cat is after the fish.
- The mouse is after the cheese.

Hold up pages 152–154 for all to see, point to the appropriate pictures, and say

- The hog comes in to catch the dog.
- The hog eats cake.
- The cow comes in.
- The cow dances with a mop.
- The sheep comes in to stop the cow.
- The sheep gets tangled in yarn.

Then ask children these questions:

PREPRODUCTION/EARLY PRODUCTION

- Is there a fly in the house? (no)
- Is there a mouse in the house? (yes)
- Does the cat or the dog go after the fish? (cat)

SPEECH EMERGENCE/INTERMEDIATE FLUENCY

- Which animal dances with a mop? (cow)
- What does the dog do when it tries to catch the cat? (The dog breaks a dish.)
- What does the hog do when it comes in to catch the dog? (The hog eats cake.)
- What happens to the sheep when it tries to stop the cow? (It gets tangled in yarn.)

BEFORE READING PAGES 155–162

Look at the illustrations on pages 155–162 with children. Then hold up pages 155–158 for all to see, point to the appropriate pictures, and say

- The hen comes in from the barn.
- The hen lays eggs on the table.
- The horse comes in.
- The horse kicks a hole in the wall.
- The elephant comes in to get rid of all the animals. The elephant is big.
- The elephant squeezes through the door.
- There is no room for anyone else.

Hold up pages 159–162 for all to see, point to the appropriate pictures, and say

- The cat and the cow leave the house.
- The horse, the hen, and the hog go out.
- The sheep walks out.
- The dog runs out.
- Then they hear a shout.
- The elephant says, "EEK! There's a mouse in the house!"

Then ask children these questions:

PREPRODUCTION/EARLY PRODUCTION

- Do all the animals leave the house at the end of the story? (no)
- Does the mouse stay in the house? (yes)
- Who shouts at the end of the story, the elephant or the mouse? (the elephant)

SPEECH EMERGENCE/INTERMEDIATE FLUENCY

- What happens when the elephant comes in the house? (Possible responses: There is no more room. The other animals leave.)
- What happens when the elephant sees the mouse? (The elephant shouts, "EEK! There's a mouse in the house!")

Harcourt Brace School Publishers

READING THE LITERATURE Have children join the Strategic Reading group and read the selection with English-fluent partners.

Responding to the Literature

TIPS FOR CLASSROOM MANAGEMENT

IF children need additional support, **THEN** complete Working with "EEK! There's a Mouse in the House" on page T277 in the *Warm Friends* Teacher's Edition.

COMPREHENSION CHECK

All Levels These questions can serve as models to meet the needs of the various language levels of your children.

PREPRODUCTION Can a cow dance with a mop? (no) Can a dog break a dish? (yes)

EARLY PRODUCTION Is this a funny story or a sad story? (funny) Which animal is afraid of the mouse in the house, the cat or the elephant? (elephant)

SPEECH EMERGENCE What animals come into the house? (mouse, cat, dog, hog, cow, sheep, hen, horse, elephant)

INTERMEDIATE FLUENCY How do you know that the elephant is afraid of the mouse? (Possible responses: He shouts; he is sweating; he is backed up against the wall.)

SURPRISE!

All Levels Form small groups and have children review the exclamatory words and phrases on each page, such as *EEK!* and *Oh my!* Ask them to write these and other expressions that people say in surprise on chart paper. Children can act out being surprised as they say the words. LISTENING/SPEAKING/WRITING

Surprise!   EEK!   Yikes!
Uh-oh!   Hey!   Oh my!
Wow!   Oh no!   Goodness!

RIDDLES AND RHYMES

Early Production/Speech Emergence Invite children to answer the following animal riddles:

- I have four legs. I bark. My name rhymes with *hog.* What am I? (dog)
- I am tiny. I squeak. My name rhymes with *house.* What am I? (mouse)

Invite children to make up their own animal riddles. Have volunteers take turns reciting their riddles to each other. LISTENING/SPEAKING

WRITING STORIES

Speech Emergence/Intermediate Fluency Have children imagine that all the animals who left the house return to help the elephant. Suggest that they write about what happens. Ask children to read their stories aloud. LISTENING/READING/WRITING

ESL/TITLE I LIBRARY
Do You Want to Be My Friend? by Eric Carle. HarperCollins, 1976. A lonely mouse searches for a playmate. **Available on ESL/Title I Audiocassette.**

SCHOOL ↔ HOME CONNECTION
Have children take home their stories and read them to family members. Ask them to report back about the parts of the stories that their families enjoyed the most.

Harcourt Brace School Publishers

Introducing the Literature

The Little Red Hen

BUILDING BACKGROUND

Prior Knowledge
Talk with children about the importance of helping family members and friends. Encourage them to tell about ways they help at home and in school. Guide children to understand that we show people we care about them when we offer to help them.

TPR: Total Physical Response
Demonstrate the sounds and actions of each of the characters in "Little Red Hen"—hen, duck, pig, and cat. Then name each animal and have children act like that animal. To extend the concept of helping people, invite volunteers to help you act out a scene in which family members or friends help each other. Then invite partners to act out their own scene as you say *May I help you?* and *Thank you.*

Develop Oral Language
Display the following rhyme, and read it aloud. Then invite volunteers to read the rhyme with you several times. You may want to point to pictures in "The Little Red Hen" that depict planting seeds, cutting and threshing wheat, grinding grains, and using flour to make bread.

> Today I'll plant some little seeds.
> That's just what I will do!
> Who will help me plant the seeds?
> Will you? Will you? Will YOU?
>
> Today I'll cut the wheat so tall.
> I'll thresh the wheat and grind grains, too.
> Who will help me do this work?
> Will you? Will you? Will YOU?
>
> Today I'll use the flour I made.
> I'll make some bread so soft and new.
> Who will help me make the bread?
> Will you? Will you? Will YOU?

BUILDING CONCEPTS

POSTER

Use Poster 17: "Making Bread"
Poster 17 shows how to make bread. Help children figure out the steps. First, wheat seeds are planted. Next, the wheat is cut. Then, the wheat is threshed and the grains are ground into flour. Last, the flour is mixed and the bread is baked. Point out that the hen is working hard. Ask how her friends could help. (They could plant seeds, cut and thresh wheat, grind grain, and mix flour.)

Write these concept words from "The Little Red Hen" on the board: *seeds, plant, wheat, cut, thresh, grind, grains, flour, bread.* Use pantomime and pictures to reinforce the meanings of unfamiliar words.

Rereading
Reread the rhyme with children, and invite volunteers to point to pictures on Poster 17 that show each part of the rhyme.

MEETING INDIVIDUAL NEEDS

Early Production Display Poster 17. Point to the wheat seeds and say what they are. Point to the bread and say what it is. Then have volunteers point to these things as you say them.

Copying Master
Use page 67 to help make the concepts more comprehensible.

TIPS FOR CLASSROOM MANAGEMENT

You may want to have children read a translation of "The Little Red Hen" in their first language with family members. See *Anthology Translation Booklets.*

Harcourt Brace School Publishers

The Little Red Hen

A. Tell a partner how to make bread. Use the pictures and the words.

seeds   plant   wheat   cut

thresh   grind   grains   flour   bread

B. Share this page with your family.

To prepare children to read "The Little Red Hen," use page 68 to provide additional concepts and language.

BEFORE READING PAGES 14–23

Read the title of the story, and then look through the illustrations on pages 14–23 with children. Hold up pages 14–15 for all to see, and say

- This is a pig. This is a cat.
- This is a duck. This is a little red hen.
- These are her baby chicks.
- The animals are friends.

Hold up pages 16–19 for all to see, and say

- The hen finds some seeds.
- The hen asks her friends to help plant seeds. Her friends will not help.
- They want to play.

Hold up pages 20–21 for all to see, and say

- The hen plants the seeds.
- The seeds grow into wheat.

Pantomime how the hen plants the seeds. Then hold up pages 22–23 for all to see, and say

- The hen asks her friends to help cut the wheat. Her friends will not help.
- They want to play.
- The hen cuts the wheat.

Pantomime how the hen cuts the wheat. Then ask children these questions:

PREPRODUCTION/EARLY PRODUCTION

- What does the hen find? (seeds)
- Do the pig, the duck, and the cat help plant the seeds? (no)

SPEECH EMERGENCE/INTERMEDIATE FLUENCY

- Who are the hen's friends? (the pig, the duck, the cat)
- Why don't the animals help the hen plant seeds? (They want to play.)

BEFORE READING PAGES 24–32

Look through the pictures on pages 24–32 with children. Then hold up pages 24–25 for all to see, and say

- The hen asks her friends to help thresh the wheat. Her friends will not help.
- The hen threshes the wheat.

Pantomime the hen threshing wheat. Then hold up pages 26–27, and say

- The hen asks her friends to help grind the grains. Her friends will not help.
- The hen grinds the grains of wheat.
- She makes flour.

Pantomime the hen grinding the grains. Then hold up pages 28–29, and say

- The hen asks her friends to help make bread. Her friends will not help.
- The hen makes the bread.

Pantomime the hen mixing the bread. Then hold up pages 30–32 for all to see, and say

- The hen asks who will help eat the bread.
- Her friends all want to help.
- The hen says no.
- The hen and her chicks eat the bread.

Then ask children these questions:

PREPRODUCTION/EARLY PRODUCTION

- Do the hen's friends help her at all? (no)
- Who makes the bread, the hen or her friends? (the hen)

SPEECH EMERGENCE/INTERMEDIATE FLUENCY

- Why wouldn't the hen let her friends eat the bread? (They didn't help make it.)
- Who would you like for a friend—the hen, the pig, the duck, or the cat? Why? (Responses will vary.)

READING THE LITERATURE Have children join the Strategic Reading group and read the selection with English-fluent partners.

Harcourt Brace School Publishers

Responding to the Literature

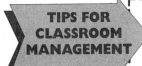

TIPS FOR CLASSROOM MANAGEMENT

IF children need additional support, **THEN** complete Working with "The Little Red Hen" on page T49 in the *Full Sails* Teacher's Edition.

COMPREHENSION CHECK

All Levels These questions can serve as models to meet the needs of the various language levels of your children.

PRE/EARLY PRODUCTION The hen works very hard in this story. Do the pig, the duck, and the cat work hard? (no) Do the animals play or eat while the hen works? (play)

SPEECH EMERGENCE What do the pig, the duck, and the cat say each time the hen asks them to help her with her work? ("Not I.") Who does the hen share the bread with? (her chicks)

INTERMEDIATE FLUENCY Do you think the pig, the duck, and the cat are good friends to the hen? Why or why not? (Possible response: No, they only wanted to help when the hen had something good to eat.)

A HELPING CHART

All Levels Tell children about some classroom activities that are planned for the next few days. Then invite children to work in small groups. Have them brainstorm ways that they can help in the classroom. As volunteers respond, make a Ways to Help chart to display in the classroom. LISTENING/SPEAKING/WRITING

Ways to Help
1. Put books away.
2. Clean up.
3. Give out papers.

DRAWING PICTURES

Early Production/Speech Emergence Invite children to draw a picture that shows their favorite part of the story. Have small groups of children gather to display their pictures and talk about them. You may want children to add their pictures to their portfolios. LISTENING/SPEAKING

LANGUAGE EXPERIENCE

Speech Emergence/Intermediate Fluency Work with children to create a new story based on the ideas in "The Little Red Hen." Suggest that they change the story so that the pig, the duck, and the cat help the hen. Talk about how the story would end. Write their version on chart paper as they dictate it. Invite children to illustrate the story, and display it on a classroom wall. LISTENING/SPEAKING

TRADE BOOK
Pancakes for Breakfast by Tomie dePaola. Harcourt Brace, 1978. In this story told in pictures, a woman tries unsuccessfully to make pancakes.

SCHOOL ↔ HOME CONNECTION
Encourage children to retell "The Little Red Hen" to their family in their own words. Have children take home their pictures to help them tell about their favorite part.

Harcourt Brace School Publishers

Introducing the Literature

BUILDING BACKGROUND

Prior Knowledge

Use pictures to lead a discussion about farm animals. Include in your discussion the names of the animals from "Henny Penny." Point out that *cock* is another name for *rooster.* Encourage children to share in their first language the sounds the animals make.

TPR: Total Physical Response

Tell children that in the story they will be reading, a hen gets hit on the head with an acorn. Act out a reaction to getting hit on your head. Then tell children that they are going to pretend that the acorn hit them, but that they must listen as you name a part of the body that the acorn hit. Provide several examples, such as the following, before children act out your directions:

Goodness me! The acorn hit your knee! *(grab knee and rub)*

Oh my! The acorn hit your eye! *(cover eye and moan)*

Develop Oral Language

Display the following rhyme, and read it aloud. Then invite volunteers to read the rhyme with you several times as they clap out the beat. You may want to point to pictures in "Henny Penny" to help children visualize the words *acorn, head, sky, falling, king,* and *fox.*

> There was a little chicken,
> whose name was Henny Penny.
> She was a silly chicken,
> with little sense—if any!
> She thought the sky was falling,
> When an acorn hit her head.
> She hurried to tell the king,
> But met a fox instead!

BUILDING CONCEPTS

Use Poster 18: "A Visit to the King"

Poster 18 shows a visit to the king.

Point to the actions on the poster, and describe what is happening. Then have volunteers point out the hen and the king. Ask what the king is wearing. (a robe) Ask where the king lives. (in a palace) Then ask what the hen is showing the king. (an acorn) Encourage volunteers to tell what the hen might be saying to the king. ("The sky is falling! It hit me on the head!")

Write these concept words from "Henny Penny" on the board: *acorn, head, sky, falling, king, hurried, palace, robe.* Use each word in a sentence to clarify its meaning. Point to each word as you read.

Rereading

Reread the rhyme with children. Invite volunteers to demonstrate actions they see pictured on Poster 18 or in "Henny Penny."

Speech Emergence Explain that chickens are farm animals. Invite children to name other animals that live on a farm. If possible, display pictures of the animals they name.

Copying Master

Use page 71 to help make the concepts more comprehensible.

TIPS FOR CLASSROOM MANAGEMENT

You may want to have children read a translation of "Henny Penny" in their first language with family members. See *Anthology Translation Booklets.*

Harcourt Brace School Publishers

Henny Penny

A. Finish each picture. Talk about it.

king

palace

robe

acorn

B. Talk to a partner about each word. Use each word to help you tell about the story.

hurried

falling

head

C. Share this page with your family.

TIPS FOR CLASSROOM MANAGEMENT To prepare children to read "Henny Penny," use page 72 to provide additional concepts and language.

BEFORE READING PAGES 38–45

Read the title and list of characters on pages 38 and 39. Point out that this is a play that can be acted out. Invite children to look through the illustrations on pages 40–44. Then hold up pages 40–41, and say

- This is Henny Penny. She is a chicken.
- She is under a tree. This is an acorn.
- An acorn falls from the tree.
- The acorn hits Henny Penny on the head.
- She thinks the sky is falling.
- She hurries to tell the king.

Pantomime Henny Penny hurrying off. Then hold up pages 42–45 for all to see, and say

- Henny Penny meets some friends.
- They are all birds.
- This is Cocky Locky. This is Ducky Lucky.
- This is Goosey Loosey. This is Turkey Lurkey.
- Henny Penny tells her friends the sky is falling.
- Henny Penny hurries to tell the king.

Then ask children these questions:

PREPRODUCTION/EARLY PRODUCTION

- Does an acorn hit Henny Penny? (yes)
- Is Henny Penny going to see the duck? (no)
- Is Henny Penny in a hurry? (yes)

SPEECH EMERGENCE/INTERMEDIATE FLUENCY

- Where is Henny Penny going? (to see the king) Why? (to tell him the sky is falling)
- Do you think the other animals believe that the sky is falling? Why or why not? (Possible response: Yes, because they go with Henny Penny to see the king.)

BEFORE READING PAGES 46–53

Ask children to look through the illustrations on pages 46–53. Then hold up pages 46–47, and say

- Henny Penny and her friends meet Foxy Loxy.
- The birds tell Foxy Loxy they are going to see the king.
- Foxy Loxy says they are going the wrong way.
- Foxy Loxy shows them a path into the woods.
- At last they reach the palace.

Hold up pages 48–49 for all to see, and say

- Foxy Loxy tries to trick the birds.
- Foxy Loxy pretends he is the king.
- Henny Penny sees his red tail.
- Henny Penny tells the other birds to run.

Hold up pages 50–51 for all to see, and say

- Foxy Loxy wants to eat the birds.
- The birds are scared.

Hold up pages 52–53 for all to see, and say

- Henny Penny wakes up. She was dreaming.
- Another acorn falls on her head.
- She thinks the sky is falling again.
- She wants to tell the king.

Then ask children these questions:

PREPRODUCTION/EARLY PRODUCTION

- Do the birds get to the palace? (yes)
- Who plays a trick, Foxy Loxy or Henny Penny? (Foxy Loxy)

SPEECH EMERGENCE/INTERMEDIATE FLUENCY

- Why do Henny Penny and the other birds go into the woods? (Foxy Loxy tells them it is the way to the palace.)
- Who pretends to be the king? (Foxy Loxy)

READING THE LITERATURE Have children join the Strategic Reading group and read the selection with English-fluent partners.

Responding to the Literature

TIPS FOR CLASSROOM MANAGEMENT

IF children need additional support, **THEN** complete Working with "Henny Penny" on page T93 in the *Full Sails* Teacher's Edition.

COMPREHENSION CHECK

All Levels These questions can serve as models to meet the needs of the various language levels of your children.

PREPRODUCTION Does the sky fall on Henny Penny? (no)

EARLY PRODUCTION What falls on Henny Penny's head, a leaf or an acorn? (an acorn)

SPEECH EMERGENCE What does Foxy Loxy wear to fool the birds? (the king's robe) Where does the king live? (in the palace)

INTERMEDIATE FLUENCY Why does Foxy Loxy dress up like the king? (Possible responses: He wants to trick the birds; he wants to eat them.) Why do you think Foxy Loxy told the birds to take the path through the woods? (Possible response: That path was the long way to the palace. He would take the short path and get there first.)

ACT OUT THE STORY

All Levels Remind children that "Henny Penny" is written like a play. Then invite children to work in groups to read the story as Readers Theatre. Before the children rehearse the story, have them decide on the parts they will play. Encourage them to use expression as they read. LISTENING/READING

PANTOMIME AN ANIMAL

Early Production/Speech Emergence Help children identify the animals in this story as a chicken, a rooster, a duck, a goose, a turkey, and a fox. Then invite children to choose one of the animals and imitate how it acts and sounds in real life. Encourage classmates to guess the names of the animals. LISTENING/SPEAKING

WRITING A STORY

Speech Emergence/Intermediate Fluency Remind children that most of the animals in this story are farm animals. Then work with them to create a new story using animals that live in the water, such as a fish, clam, and lobster. Children can make up names for these characters, such as Clammy Sammy. Have children draw pictures to illustrate their stories. WRITING

 ESL/TITLE I LIBRARY
You Silly Goose by Ellen Stoll Walsh. Harcourt Brace, 1996. After jumping to conclusions too quickly, Lulu the goose finds herself in trouble. **Available on ESL/Title I Audiocassette.**

SCHOOL ↔ HOME CONNECTION
Encourage children to take home their story. Have them retell the story to family members and report back about how family members liked the story.

Harcourt Brace School Publishers

Introducing the Literature

Little Lumpty

BUILDING BACKGROUND

Prior Knowledge

Recite the nursery rhyme "Humpty Dumpty" for children, inviting them to join in. Encourage children to share other nursery rhymes or nonsense rhymes from their native countries.

TPR: Total Physical Response

To further develop children's knowledge of "Humpty Dumpty," act out the rhyme while you recite it. Then repeat the rhyme several times, and have children follow your directions to act it out.

Develop Oral Language

Display the following rhyme, and read it aloud. Then invite volunteers to read the rhyme with you several times, emphasizing the rhyming words. You may want to point to the following illustrations in "Little Lumpty": Little Lumpty, wall, ladder, danced, dark.

> Humpty Dumpty
>   had a great fall.
> Then Little Lumpty
>   climbed the same wall.
> What did he use?
> A ladder so tall!
>
> Little Lumpty
>   danced on the wall.
> Then it got dark,
>   and he thought he would fall.
> Who helped him then?
> His friends, one and all!

BUILDING CONCEPTS

Use Poster 19: "Humpty Dumpty and Little Lumpty"

Poster 19 shows Humpty Dumpty and Little Lumpty on the same town wall. Help children compare the scenes. Point out that the wall is the same. Use Poster 19 to help children talk about the differences and similarities between Humpty Dumpty and Little Lumpty.

Write these concept words from "Little Lumpty" on the board: *town, wall, fall, ladder, danced, dark, blanket, bounced*. Draw pictures to illustrate the meanings of some of the words.

Rereading

Reread the rhyme with children, and invite volunteers to point to any concept words they see pictured on Poster 19 or in "Little Lumpty."

MEETING INDIVIDUAL NEEDS

Challenge Invite children to name words that rhyme with *wall*.

Copying Master

Use page 75 to help make the concepts more comprehensible.

TIPS FOR CLASSROOM MANAGEMENT

You may want to have children read a translation of "Little Lumpty" in their first language with family members. See *Anthology Translation Booklets*.

Harcourt Brace School Publishers

Little Lumpty

A. Work with a partner. Finish each sentence.

fall

The Rules of the Town of Dumpty

_____

- - - - - - - - - - - - - - - -

❶ Do not sit on the _____ .

_____

- - - - - - - - - - - - - - - -

You might _____ down.

_____

- - - - - - - - - - - - - - - -

bounced

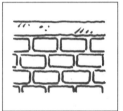

wall

❷ Do not use a _____ to climb

up the wall.

_____

- - - - - - - - - - - - - - - -

dark

❸ No playing after _____ .

❹ Do not cover the wall with a

_____

- - - - - - - - - - - - - - - -

_____ .

_____

- - - - - - - - - - - - - - - -

ladder

❺ Balls cannot be _____ on

the wall.

blanket

B. Draw a poster of one of the rules above.

C. Share this page with family members.

TIPS FOR CLASSROOM MANAGEMENT To prepare children to read "Little Lumpty," use page 76 to provide them with additional concepts and language.

BEFORE READING PAGES 62–71

Read aloud the title, and invite children to look at the illustrations on pages 62–71. Then hold up pages 64–65 for all to see, and say

- This is the town of Dumpty.
- Humpty Dumpty lived here.

Hold up pages 66–67 for all to see, and say

- This is Little Lumpty.
- This is Little Lumpty's mother.
- They live in the town of Dumpty.
- Lumpty loves Humpty Dumpty's wall.
- He climbs up the wall. He uses a ladder.

Pantomime Lumpty carrying the ladder, placing it against the wall, and climbing up. Then hold up pages 68–69 for all to see, and say

- The wall is high. Lumpty sees his house.
- Lumpty sees his school.
- Lumpty dances on the wall.

Pantomime Lumpty dancing. Then hold up pages 70–71, and say

- Lumpty looks down. He gets scared.

Then ask children these questions:

PREPRODUCTION/EARLY PRODUCTION

- Does Little Lumpty live in the town of Dumpty? (yes)
- What does Little Lumpty climb, a tree or a wall? (wall)

SPEECH EMERGENCE/INTERMEDIATE FLUENCY

- Why does Lumpty get scared? (Possible responses: The wall is high; he looks down.)
- What do you think Lumpty will do next? (Possible response: He might look for the ladder and try to get down.)

BEFORE READING PAGES 72–81

Hold up pages 72–73 for all to see, and say

- Lumpty cannot get to the ladder.
- It gets dark.
- Lumpty thinks about Humpty Dumpty.

Hold up pages 74–75 for all to see, and say

- Lumpty screams for help.
- People come out of their houses.

Act out a person running from his or her house and asking what is wrong. Then hold up pages 76–79 for all to see, and say

- Lumpty's mother gets a blanket.
- The people stretch the blanket.
- They tell Lumpty to jump.
- He bounces on the blanket. He is safe.

Use your hands to pantomime Lumpty bouncing on the blanket three times. Then hold up pages 80–81 for all to see, and say

- Lumpty says he is sorry.
- He goes home with his mother.
- He goes to bed. He whispers to the moon.
- He says he still loves the wall.

Then ask children these questions:

PREPRODUCTION/EARLY PRODUCTION

- Is Lumpty safe at the end of the story? (yes)
- Who helps save Lumpty, his father or mother? (mother)

SPEECH EMERGENCE/INTERMEDIATE FLUENCY

- How does the blanket help Lumpty? (He jumps on the blanket and bounces. He lands safely.)
- What would you have done if you were Lumpty? (Responses will vary.)

Harcourt Brace School Publishers

READING THE LITERATURE Have children join the Strategic Reading group and read the selection with English-fluent partners.

Responding to the Literature

TIPS FOR CLASSROOM MANAGEMENT

IF children need additional support, **THEN** complete Working with "Little Lumpty" on page T149 in the *Full Sails* Teacher's Edition.

COMPREHENSION CHECK

All Levels These questions can serve as models to meet the needs of the various language levels of your children.

PREPRODUCTION Does Lumpty climb the wall? (yes)

EARLY PRODUCTION Who brings the blanket? (mother) Does Lumpty still love the wall? (yes)

SPEECH EMERGENCE What did Lumpty say to his mother after he got down? ("I'm sorry.")

INTERMEDIATE FLUENCY Why do you think Lumpty said he was sorry? (Possible response: He did not listen to his mother.) Do you think it was a good idea for Lumpty to climb the wall? Why or why not? (Responses will vary.)

SURVEYING CLASSMATES

All Levels Ask children to think about whether Lumpty might ever climb the wall again. Then help children create a survey chart similar to the one below. Assign three sets of partners who will survey students. Have partners ask whether Lumpty might climb the wall again. Combine the results of the surveys into a group chart. LISTENING/SPEAKING

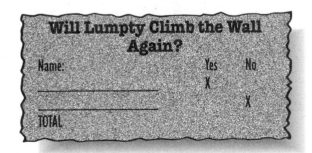

Will Lumpty Climb the Wall Again?

Name:	Yes	No
	X	
		X
TOTAL		

ACTING OUT

Early Production/Speech Emergence Remind children that at the end of the story, Little Lumpty tells his mother that he is sorry. Ask children to tell what they think Little Lumpty's mother said in reply. Model some safety rules that Lumpty's mother might say, for example, *It is dangerous to climb a wall* or *Never use a ladder by yourself!* Then encourage partners to act out this scene. LISTENING/SPEAKING

LANGUAGE EXPERIENCE

Speech Emergence/Intermediate Fluency
Invite children to pretend that Lumpty has a little brother. Then work with them to create a new story about Lumpty's little brother. As children tell what happens, write the story on chart paper. Then invite each child to illustrate the story. WRITING

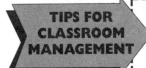 **ESL/TITLE I LIBRARY**
Deep in the Forest by Brinton Turkle. Dutton Children's Books, 1976. In this twist on the Goldilocks story, a mischievous bear enters the cabin of a pioneer family out for a walk.

SCHOOL ↔ HOME CONNECTION
Invite children to take home the pictures they drew and tell their new story to family members.

Introducing the Literature

The Wild Woods

BUILDING BACKGROUND

Prior Knowledge
Talk with children about how to care for pets. Help them understand that pets need food, water, love, and care. Encourage them to name animals that make good pets, such as dogs, cats, and goldfish. Then ask children to name animals that are not good pets, such as deer, bears, or squirrels. Help them understand that these animals are wild.

TPR: Total Physical Response
To develop the concept of pets and wild animals further, write the words *Wild Animal* on one large card and *Pet* on another. As you hold up and read a card, act like an animal that fits the category on the card. Help children guess the name. After demonstrating several times with both cards, read and hold up a card, then call on volunteers to respond by acting appropriately.

Develop Oral Language
Display the following rhyme and read it aloud. Talk about why the speaker of the poem could not care for a wild squirrel in the ways named. Then have children read the rhyme with you several times. You may want to pantomime the word *sleep* and use pictures in "The Wild Woods" to help children visualize the words *woods, Grandad, squirrel,* and *sandwiches*.

> Grandad and I went for a walk
> In the wild woods very deep.
> A squirrel jumped out and looked at me.
> I wanted to take him home to keep.
>
> "What will he eat?" Grandad asked.
> "Can you take care of a wild thing?"
> "I'll feed him sandwiches," I said.
> "And he'll sleep in my room like a king!"

BUILDING CONCEPTS

Use Poster 20: "Pets and Wild Animals"
Poster 20 shows pets and wild animals. Invite children to name the animals and tell how the groups of animals are different. Ask a volunteer to point to Grandad and tell how Grandad cares for his pets. (feeds goldfish, takes dog for walk) Invite volunteers to point to some wild animals. (deer, squirrel, fox) Use Poster 20 to help children talk about animals.

Write these concept words from "The Wild Woods" on the board, and read aloud as you talk about each one: *woods, Grandad, squirrel, wild, care, sandwiches, sleep.*

Rereading
Invite children to reread the rhyme with you. Have volunteers point to any illustrations of concept words that they see on Poster 20 or in "The Wild Woods."

MEETING INDIVIDUAL NEEDS

Extra Support Invite children to draw pictures of their favorite pet and their favorite wild animal. Display the pictures in the classroom.

Copying Master
Use page 79 to help make the concepts more comprehensible.

TIPS FOR CLASSROOM MANAGEMENT

You may want to have children read a translation of "The Wild Woods" in their first language with family members. See *Anthology Translation Booklets.*

Harcourt Brace School Publishers

AME _____

The Wild Woods

A. Walk around the classroom. Talk with your friends.

Find someone who

❶ has walked in the woods.

_____

- -

_____

❷ lives near his or her grandad.

_____

- -

_____

❸ has seen a squirrel.

_____

- -

_____

❹ likes to eat sandwiches.

_____

- -

_____

❺ has a pet.

_____

- -

_____

B. Share this page with your family.

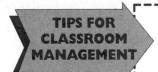

To prepare children to read "The Wild Woods," use page 80 to provide additional concepts and language.

BEFORE READING PAGES 90–97

Read aloud the story title, and invite children to look at the illustrations on pages 90–97. Then hold up pages 92–93 for all to see, and say

- This is Jess. This is Grandad.
- They are talking a walk. This is a squirrel.
- Jess wants to take the squirrel home.
- Grandad says the squirrel is wild.
- Jess follows the squirrel into the woods.
- Grandad follows Jess.

Hold up pages 94–95 for all to see, and say

- Grandad asks what Jess would feed the squirrel.
- Jess thinks she can feed it sandwiches.

Pantomime Grandad trying to keep up with Jess. Then hold up pages 96–97, and say

- Grandad asks where the squirrel will sleep.
- Jess says it could sleep in her room.
- Jess follows the squirrel.
- Grandad follows Jess.

Pantomime Grandad wringing out his wet clothes and stepping through the mud. Then ask children these questions:

PREPRODUCTION/EARLY PRODUCTION

- Does Jess see a cat? (no)
- Does Jess see a squirrel? (yes)
- Do you like squirrels? (yes/no)
- Are Jess and Grandad walking in a town or in the woods? (woods)

SPEECH EMERGENCE/INTERMEDIATE FLUENCY

- What does Jess want to do with the squirrel? (take it home)
- Do you think Jess will take the squirrel home? Why or why not? (Possible response: No, Grandad won't let her.)

BEFORE READING PAGES 98–102

Look through the illustrations on pages 98–102 with children. Then hold up pages 98–99 for all to see, and say

- Jess stops walking.
- She looks at a waterfall.
- Grandad is resting.

Hold up pages 100–101 for all to see, and say

- Grandad tells Jess that she can't keep a squirrel.
- Jess knows that.
- A squirrel belongs in the wild.
- Jess likes being in the woods.
- She wants to come back tomorrow.

Hold up page 102 for all to see, and say

- These are ducks.
- Jess wants to come back.
- She says one of the ducks might need to be taken care of.

Then ask children these questions:

PREPRODUCTION/EARLY PRODUCTION

- Do Jess and Grandad sit in a house? (no)
- Do Jess and Grandad sit near a waterfall? (yes)
- Do Jess and Grandad see ducks or frogs at the end of the story? (ducks)

SPEECH EMERGENCE/INTERMEDIATE FLUENCY

- When does Jess want to go back to the woods? (tomorrow)
- Why wouldn't a duck from the woods make a good pet? (Possible responses: It is wild; it belongs in the woods.)
- How do you think Grandad felt as he sat near the waterfall? Why? (Responses will vary.)

Harcourt Brace School Publishers

READING THE LITERATURE Have children join the Strategic Reading group and read the selection with English-fluent partners.

Responding to the Literature

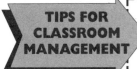
TIPS FOR CLASSROOM MANAGEMENT

IF children need additional support, **THEN** complete Working with "The Wild Woods" on page T209 in the *Full Sails* Teacher's Edition.

COMPREHENSION CHECK

All Levels These questions can serve as models to meet the needs of the various language levels of your children.

EARLY PRODUCTION Does Jess walk in the woods? (yes) Does she take the squirrel home? (no)
SPEECH EMERGENCE Where do Jess and Grandad stop to rest? (by a waterfall) Where did they see the wild animals? (in the woods)
INTERMEDIATE FLUENCY Why does Jess want to go back to the woods? (Possible response: She thinks one of the ducks may need care.) Do you agree that Jess should not keep a wild animal? Why or why not? (Possible responses: Yes, wild animals belong outside; wild animals do not make good pets.)

A WALK IN THE WOODS MURAL

All Levels Invite children to brainstorm things they might see in the woods. You may wish to provide books that show woodland scenes. Then have small groups create sections of a mural showing the woods. Provide each group with butcher paper, and ask children to draw plants, trees, and wild animals. Encourage children to talk to each other about what they are drawing and to label the plants or animals. Tape the sections together, and display the mural. LISTENING/SPEAKING/WRITING

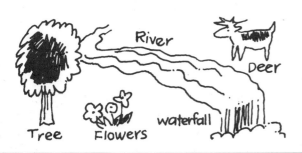

WHERE'S MY HOME?

Early Production/Speech Emergence Play a game of "Where Is My Home?" Name a wild animal or a pet. Then ask children to tell where that animal lives. You might say, *I am a fox. Where is my home?* (in the woods) After modeling the game for children, encourage them to play it in pairs or small groups. LISTENING/SPEAKING

WRITING A STORY

Speech Emergence/Intermediate Fluency Invite children to think of a story about walking in the woods and seeing a wild animal. Have them draw pictures to show what would happen at the beginning, in the middle, and at the end of the story. Encourage them to write about the pictures. Children can use their pictures to help them tell the story aloud. WRITING

ESL/TITLE I LIBRARY
Growing Colors by Bruce McMillan. Mulberry, 1988. This collection of photographs teaches how fruits and vegetables grow. **Available on ESL/Title I Audiocassette.**

SCHOOL ↔ HOME CONNECTION
Encourage children to take home their picture stories and share them with family members. Have them report back about how family members liked their stories.

Harcourt Brace School Publishers

Wonderful Worms

BUILDING BACKGROUND

Prior Knowledge

Discuss children's knowledge of worms. Talk about where worms live, why we need worms, and how children feel about worms. Encourage children to share what worms are called in their first language.

TPR: Total Physical Response

To develop the concept of worms further, use one hand to demonstrate how an earthworm might move along your arm. Invite children to mimic the movement. Then tell students to act like a worm when you say "stretch and squeeze." They should reach high into the air to stretch and squat to squeeze. Then say "wiggle," and have them respond by wiggling their bodies.

Develop Oral Language

Display the following rhyme. Read it aloud, emphasizing the beat. Then encourage children to read the rhyme with you as you repeat it several times. You may want to move your hands and arms to show the following words: *short, fat, long, thin.*

Worms. Worms. Wonderful worms!
Worms live in the earth below.
Short and fat, long and thin —
Moving rather slow.

Worms. Worms. Wiggly worms!
They dig in the soil below.
They make the dirt so nice and soft,
So all my flowers can grow!

BUILDING CONCEPTS

Use Poster 21: "A Home for Worms"

Poster 21 depicts earthworms in their environment. Have volunteers point to worms in the picture. Ask what worms do in the dirt. (dig) Ask volunteers what a worm might do if you held it in your hand. (wiggle) Help children understand that as worms dig, they make the dirt soft and airy. Use the poster to talk about why worms are important to plants. (Plants grow better in dirt that is soft and airy.)

Write these concept words from "Wonderful Worms" on the board: *worms, fat, wiggly, long, thin, short, dig, dirt, soil.* Use each word in a sentence to clarify its meaning.

Rereading

Invite children to reread the rhyme with you. Have volunteers point to any concept words that they see pictured on Poster 21 or in "Wonderful Worms."

MEETING INDIVIDUAL NEEDS

Preproduction Invite children to use their fingers to show how a worm wiggles through the dirt.

Copying Master

Use page 83 to help make the concepts more comprehensible.

TIPS FOR CLASSROOM MANAGEMENT

You may want to have children read a translation of "Wonderful Worms" in their first language with family members. See *Anthology Translation Booklets.*

Harcourt Brace School Publishers

Wonderful Worms

A. Tell about each worm. Use the words below the pictures.

fat   short

long   thin

B. Read the sentences with a partner. Find a word to finish each sentence.

_____

- - - - - - - - - - - - - - - - -

❶ Worms are _____.

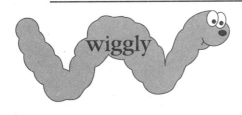

wiggly

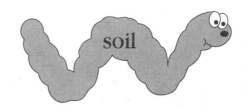

soil

_____

- - - - - - - - - - - - - - - - -

❷ Worms move in the _____.

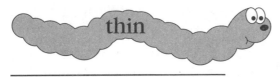

thin

dirt

_____

- - - - - - - - - - - - - - - - -

❸ Worms_____ in the soil.

short

dig

C. Share this page with your family.

TIPS FOR CLASSROOM MANAGEMENT To prepare children to read "Wonderful Worms," use page 84 to provide additional concepts and language.

BEFORE READING PAGES 110–117

Read aloud the title of the story and look through the illustrations on pages 110–117 with children. Then hold up pages 112–113 for all to see, and say

- These are a boy's hands and feet.
- This is an earthworm.
- Worms are fat and wiggly.
- Worms live in the cool, dark ground.
- These roots grow in the ground.
- This bird eats worms.

Hold up pages 114–115 for all to see, and say

- Worms can feel sounds.
- The worms feel the boy's footsteps.
- The footsteps feel like thunder.
- This is a chipmunk.
- This chipmunk lives in the ground.

Pantomime the boy walking along the ground. Then hold up pages 116–117, and say

- This is a worm's hole.
- Worms are good diggers.
- They move through dirt.
- They eat the dirt as they go.

Then ask children these questions:

PREPRODUCTION/EARLY PRODUCTION

- Do birds eat worms? (yes)
- Do you eat worms? (no)
- Are worms good diggers? (yes)

SPEECH EMERGENCE/INTERMEDIATE FLUENCY

- Worms live in the ground. What is it like underground? (cool and dark)
- What do a boy's footsteps feel like to a worm? (thunder)
- How do worms dig in the dirt? (They move through the dirt and eat it.)

BEFORE READING PAGES 118–123

Look through the illustrations on pages 118–123 with children. Then hold up pages 118–119 for all to see, and say

- Worms move in a special way.
- First they stretch out long and thin.
- Then they squeeze in short and fat.
- Worms mix the dirt as they move.
- Worms make the soil soft.
- The roots of plants like to grow in this kind of dirt.

Use your hand to show how a worm stretches and squeezes. Then hold up pages 120–121 for all to see, and say

- Worms do not have eyes, ears, or a nose.
- Worms do have a mouth.
- Worms eat dirt and leaves.
- The food changes inside the worms.
- It comes out of the worms.
- It makes the dirt good for growing plants.

Hold up pages 122–123 for all to see, and say

- Earthworms help people.
- They make the dirt nice for the flowers and plants we grow.

Then ask children these questions:

PREPRODUCTION/EARLY PRODUCTION

- Do worms have eyes? (no)
- Do worms have a mouth? (yes)
- Do worms help plants grow? (yes)

SPEECH EMERGENCE/INTERMEDIATE FLUENCY

- How do worms move? (They stretch and squeeze.)
- What do worms eat? (dirt and leaves)
- How do worms make the soil better? (Possible response: They make it soft.)

READING THE LITERATURE Have children join the Strategic Reading group and read the selection with English-fluent partners.

Harcourt Brace School Publishers

Responding to the Literature

TIPS FOR CLASSROOM MANAGEMENT

IF children need additional support, **THEN** complete Working with "Wonderful Worms" on page T261 in the *Full Sails* Teacher's Edition.

COMPREHENSION CHECK

All Levels These questions can serve as models to meet the needs of the various language levels of your children.

PREPRODUCTION Do worms help us? (yes)
EARLY PRODUCTION Where would you find a worm? (Possible responses: in the ground; in the dirt; in the soil; in the garden)
SPEECH EMERGENCE When a worm stretches, is it long and thin or short and fat? (long and thin)
INTERMEDIATE FLUENCY What do worms look like? (Possible responses: They are fat; they are long; they are wiggly; they squeeze and stretch when they move.) Why do gardeners like worms? (Possible responses: Worms make the dirt softer; worms make the dirt better for plants.)

OBSERVE AN ANIMAL

All Levels Take children for a walk in the neighborhood near your school to observe a wild animal. Caution them not to touch any wild animals. Have small groups of children take notes and draw pictures of the animal. Have volunteers report on what they observed. Create a chart to record their observations. LISTENING/SPEAKING/WRITING

How It Looks	How It Acts
furry	climbs trees
bushy tail	eats nuts
gray	makes "chattering" noise

WORMY WORDS

Early Production/Speech Emergence On index cards, write the following words: *dig, wiggle, stretch, squeeze, eat, fly, sing, hop, bark, run.* Mix up the cards and invite small groups of children to read the words aloud. Have children act out each word and then sort the words into two groups: words that tell what worms can do and words that tell what worms cannot do. LISTENING/SPEAKING

LANGUAGE EXPERIENCE

Speech Emergence/Intermediate Fluency
Have children brainstorm a list of animals. Ask them to choose one of the animals and tell a story about it. Record the story on chart paper as children dictate it. Then have children illustrate the story. Display the story. Have children use the group story to write their own fact sheets about the animal. Save their fact sheets in their portfolios. WRITING

ESL/TITLE I LIBRARY
What Do You See? by Jannina Domanska. Macmillan, 1974. Several animals describe the world from their point of view.

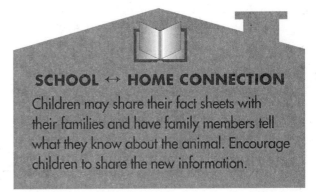

SCHOOL ↔ HOME CONNECTION
Children may share their fact sheets with their families and have family members tell what they know about the animal. Encourage children to share the new information.

Harcourt Brace School Publishers

BUILDING BACKGROUND

Prior Knowledge

Talk with children about how seeds grow into plants. Encourage them to share their knowledge of the growing process. Help them recognize that after seeds are planted in the ground they need sun, water, and care to help them grow.

TPR: Total Physical Response

To help develop children's understanding of gardening, read the following chant and pantomime the actions. Then have children join you in pantomiming as you repeat the chant several times.

First, we plant the seeds in the dirt. (*Act out planting seeds in the ground.*)

Then, we wait, wait, wait. (*Cross your arms and tap your foot.*)

Next, we water our seeds. (*Act out watering the seeds.*)

Finally, we see the beautiful flowers! (*Act surprised.*)

Then we clap, clap, clap. (*Clap your hands.*)

Develop Oral Language

Display the following rhyme, and read it aloud. Invite children to join you as you repeat the rhyme several times. Use your voice to demonstrate the word *shouted*.

> Toad planted some seeds in a garden.
> He put them deep in the ground.
> He watched for the seeds to start growing.
> He stood and he waited around.
>
> "Now seeds, start growing!" he shouted
> In a voice that made them afraid.
> But the seeds needed time, rainwater, and sun
> Before green plants could be made!

BUILDING CONCEPTS

Use Poster 22: "How Seeds Grow"

Poster 22 shows the growing process. Ask where seeds are growing. (in a garden, in the ground) Have children name two things that seeds need in order to grow. (rain, sun) Encourage children to use the pictures on Poster 22 to describe the growing process.

Write these concept words from "Frog and Toad Together" on the board, and use each one in a sentence to clarify meaning: *garden, ground, growing, shouted, afraid, sun, rain.*

Rereading

Reread the rhyme with children. Invite volunteers to point to any concept words pictured on Poster 22 or in "Frog and Toad Together."

MEETING INDIVIDUAL NEEDS

Challenge Encourage children to choose two of the concept words and use them in a sentence about seeds.

Copying Master

Use page 87 to help make the concepts more comprehensible.

TIPS FOR CLASSROOM MANAGEMENT

You may want to have children read a translation of "Frog and Toad Together" in their first language with family members. See *Anthology Translation Booklets.*

Harcourt Brace School Publishers

Frog and Toad Together

A. Work with a partner. Think about how a garden grows. Use the words to complete the flowchart.

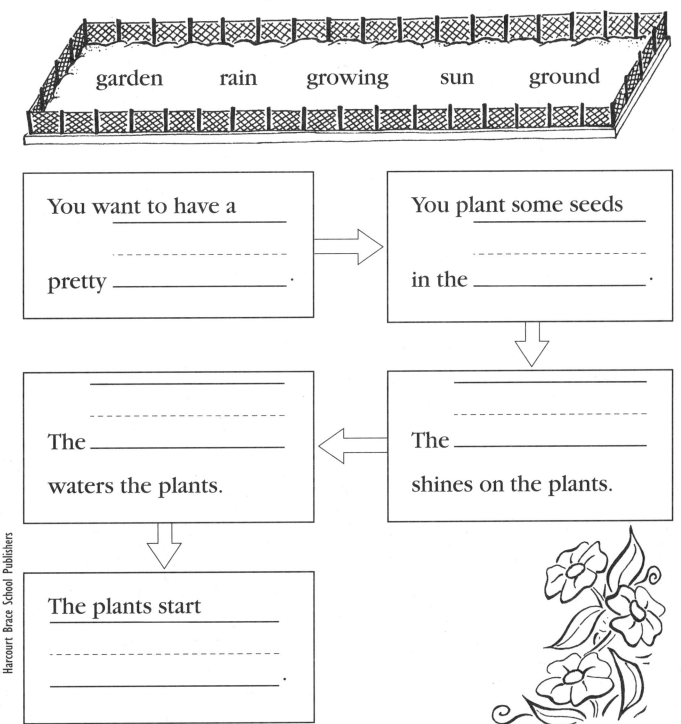

garden   rain   growing   sun   ground

You want to have a _____ ---------------------- pretty _____ .

You plant some seeds _____ ---------------------- in the _____ .

The _____ ---------------------- shines on the plants.

The _____ ---------------------- waters the plants.

The plants start _____ ---------------------- _____ .

B. Share this page with your family.

TIPS FOR CLASSROOM MANAGEMENT To prepare children to read "Frog and Toad Together," use page 88 to provide additional concepts and language.

BEFORE READING PAGES 134–143

Read aloud the title of the book. Look through the illustrations on pages 134–143 with children. Then hold up pages 136–137 for all to see, and say

- This is Frog. This is Toad.
- Frog is working in his garden.
- It is hard work.
- Toad wants a garden, too.
- Frog gives Toad some flower seeds.

Hold up pages 138–139 for all to see, and say

- Toad plants the seeds in the ground.
- He tells the seeds to start growing.
- Toad talks to the seeds in a loud voice.
- "Start growing!" he says.
- The seeds do not grow.

Act out Toad talking to the seeds. Then hold up pages 140–141, and say

- Toad shouts at the seeds.
- Frog tells Toad that he shouts too much.
- The seeds are afraid to grow.

Hold up pages 142–143, and say

- Frog says the seeds need sun.
- Frog says the seeds need rain.
- Then the seeds will start to grow.

Then ask children these questions:

PREPRODUCTION/EARLY PRODUCTION

- Does Toad plant seeds? (yes)
- Did you ever plant seeds? (yes/no)
- Who gives Toad the seeds? (Frog)

SPEECH EMERGENCE/INTERMEDIATE FLUENCY

- What does Toad want his seeds to do? (start growing)
- What do the seeds need to grow? (Possible responses: They need rain; they need sun.)

BEFORE READING PAGES 144–150

Look through the illustrations on pages 144–150 with children. Then hold up pages 144–145 for all to see, and say

- Toad looks outside. It is night.
- The seeds did not grow.
- Toad thinks the seeds are afraid of the dark.
- Toad lights some candles.
- Toad tells a story to the seeds.

Hold up pages 146–147 for all to see, and say

- The next day, Toad sings to the seeds.
- Toad reads poems to the seeds.
- Toad plays music for the seeds.
- The seeds still do not grow.
- Toad is very tired. Toad falls asleep.

Pantomime Toad's actions of singing, reading poems, playing music, and falling asleep. Then hold up page 148 for all to see, and say

- Frog wakes up Toad.
- He tells Toad to look at the garden.
- The seeds are growing.

Then ask children these questions:

PREPRODUCTION/EARLY PRODUCTION

- Do Toad's seeds grow? (yes)
- Does Toad read to the seeds? (yes)

SPEECH EMERGENCE/INTERMEDIATE FLUENCY

- What does Toad do to help his seeds grow? (He sings to them; he reads to them; he plays music for them.)
- How do you know that Frog and Toad are good friends? (Accept reasonable responses.)

READING THE LITERATURE Have children join the Strategic Reading group and read the selection with English-fluent partners.

Harcourt Brace School Publishers

Responding to the Literature

TIPS FOR CLASSROOM MANAGEMENT

IF children need additional support, **THEN** complete Working with "Frog and Toad Together" on page T311 in the *Full Sails* Teacher's Edition.

COMPREHENSION CHECK

All Levels These questions can serve as models to meet the needs of the various language levels of your children.

PREPRODUCTION Are Frog and Toad friends? (yes)

EARLY PRODUCTION Who plants seeds first, Frog or Toad? (Frog) Who says gardening is hard work? (Frog and Toad)

SPEECH EMERGENCE Why does Toad light candles and sing to his seeds? (He thinks they are afraid.) What do the seeds need to grow? (sun, rain, time)

INTERMEDIATE FLUENCY Why does Toad fall asleep? (He is tired.) How are Frog and Toad alike? How are they different? (Possible responses: They are both animals; they are both friends; Frog knows about having a garden; Toad does not.)

HOW DOES YOUR GARDEN GROW?

All Levels Point out to children that some fruits and vegetables can be grown from seeds, such as watermelons, cantaloupes, and beans. Then invite children to draw a picture of what they would grow if they had a garden. Children may want to display their pictures and describe their gardens. LISTENING/SPEAKING

ACT OUT THE STORY

Speech Emergence/Intermediate Fluency
Invite pairs of children to act out one of the scenes in the story in which Frog talks to Toad. After they practice, invite the pairs to act out the scene for their classmates. LISTENING/SPEAKING

WRITING ABOUT GARDENS

Speech Emergence/Intermediate Fluency
Invite children to write a garden story. Suggest that the story include two friends. Have children draw pictures to show what happens at the beginning, in the middle, and at the end of their story. Encourage them to write about the pictures and to tell their story to their classmates. You might want to have children put their stories in their portfolios.
LISTENING/SPEAKING/WRITING

 **ESL/TITLE I LIBRARY**
In the Tall, Tall Grass by Denise Fleming. Henry Holt, 1991. This rhyme describes a caterpillar's view of other creatures. **Available on ESL/Title I Audiocassette.**

SCHOOL ↔ HOME CONNECTION
Children can take home their garden stories and share them with their family members. Invite them to report back about how family members liked their stories.

Harcourt Brace School Publishers

Introducing the Literature

Lionel in the Winter

BUILDING BACKGROUND

Prior Knowledge

Discuss snow with children. Ask if they have seen snow. Talk about what snow looks like and feels like. Then invite children to name things that they have done or would like to do in the snow.

TPR: Total Physical Response

To further develop the concept of snow, draw a snowman on the board. Point out that building a snowman is something many children like to do when it snows. Then pantomime building a snowman, talking about how a snowman can be made from three balls of snow. Ask volunteers to help you as you call out what to do, such as *Pack the snow in your hands.* Then pretend to add things to make eyes, a nose, and arms.

Develop Oral Language

Display the following rhyme, and read it aloud. Use your hands to demonstrate *tall* and to point out your own nose, eyes, arms, and neck. Invite children to join you as you repeat the rhyme several times.

A snowman! A snowman!
A snowman so tall!
Roll up the snow.
Make a big ball.

A potato for the nose,
And marbles for the eyes,
Branches for the arms,
Reaching so high.

A scarf around the neck,
And a hat to top it all–
A snowman! A snowman!
A snowman so tall!

BUILDING CONCEPTS

 Use Poster 23: "Building a Snowman"

Poster 23 shows how to make a snowman. Talk with children about the steps in this process. Tell children that the first thing they would do to make a snowman is to roll a big ball. Ask what they would do second. (Roll a smaller ball.) Have them tell what they would do next and what they would do last. (Roll the smallest ball. Add a nose, eyes, arms, and scarf.)

Write these concept words from "Lionel in the Winter" on the board, and use each one in a sentence to clarify meaning: *snowman, ball, potato, nose, branches, arms, eyes, marbles, scarf.*

Rereading

Invite children to reread the rhyme with you again. Have volunteers point to any concept words pictured in "Lionel in the Winter."

MEETING INDIVIDUAL NEEDS

Speech Emergence Ask children to suggest other items that could be used for a snowman's eyes and nose.

Copying Master

Use page 91 to help make the concepts more comprehensible.

TIPS FOR CLASSROOM MANAGEMENT

You may want to have children read a translation of "Lionel in the Winter" in their first language with family members. See *Anthology Translation Booklets.*

Harcourt Brace School Publishers

Lionel in the Winter

A. Draw these things to finish the snowman.

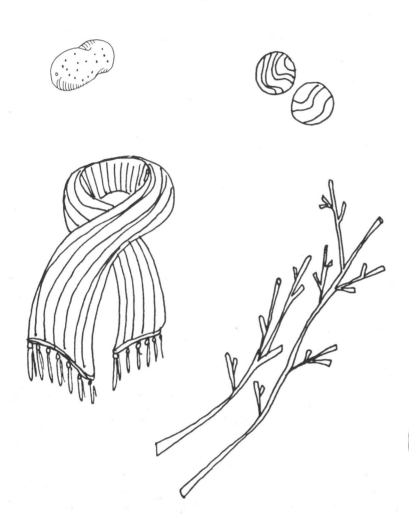

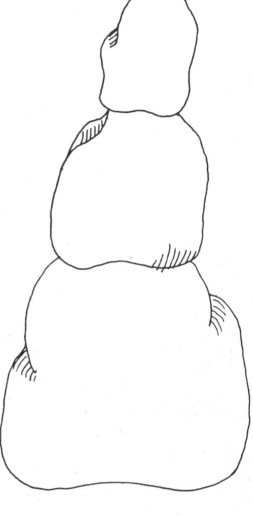

B. Tell a partner about your snowman.

What did you use for its  ?

What did you use for its  ?

What did you use for its  ?

C. Take your snowman home. Tell your family about it.

TIPS FOR CLASSROOM MANAGEMENT

To prepare children to read "Lionel in the Winter," use page 92 to provide additional concepts and language.

BEFORE READING PAGES 158–165

Read aloud the title of the story. Look through the illustrations on pages 158–165 with children. Then hold up pages 160–161, and say

- This is Lionel. This is Jeffrey.
- They are friends.
- They are building a snowman.
- They use three balls of snow.

Hold up pages 162–163 for all to see, and say

- Lionel puts a potato on the snowman for the nose.
- Lionel uses branches for the arms.
- Lionel uses marbles for the eyes.

Have children point to their own nose, eyes, and arms. Then hold up pages 164–165 for all to see, and say

- Lionel puts a hat on the snowman.
- Lionel puts a scarf on the snowman.
- The snowman is facing the house.
- Louise says the snowman should face the street.

Demonstrate the meaning of *facing* by facing the board and telling children where you are facing. Then ask children these questions:

PREPRODUCTION/EARLY PRODUCTION

- Does Lionel make a snowman? (yes)
- Does Lionel use a carrot or a potato for the nose? (potato)

SPEECH EMERGENCE/INTERMEDIATE FLUENCY

- Who helps Lionel build the snowman? (Jeffrey)
- Lionel uses a potato for the snowman's nose. What else does he use? (marbles for eyes, branches for arms, a scarf and hat)

BEFORE READING PAGES 166–171

Invite children to look at the illustrations on pages 166–171 with you. Then hold up pages 166–167 for all to see, and say

- Lionel says the snowman can watch the house.
- He says the snowman can guard the house from tigers.
- Jeffrey says that could be dangerous.

Point to the cat that Lionel calls a tiger. Then hold up pages 168–169 for all to see, and say

- Jeffrey is getting cold.
- He wants to go inside.
- Lionel looks at the snowman.
- He wonders if the snowman will be lonely.
- He can't bring the snowman inside.

Hold up pages 170–171 for all to see, and say

- Lionel and Jeffrey build more snowmen.
- They go inside for cocoa.
- Their snowman is not lonely.

Then ask children these questions:

PREPRODUCTION/EARLY PRODUCTION

- Are Lionel and Jeffrey worried about real tigers? (no)
- Does Lionel think about the snowman being lonely? (yes)

SPEECH EMERGENCE/INTERMEDIATE FLUENCY

- Why does Jeffrey want to go inside? (He is getting cold.)
- Why do Lionel and Jeffrey build more snowmen? (They don't want the first snowman to be lonely.)
- Why can't Lionel and Jeffrey bring the snowman inside? (Possible response: It will melt.)

READING THE LITERATURE   Have children join the Strategic Reading group and read the selection with English-fluent partners.

Harcourt Brace School Publishers

Responding to the Literature

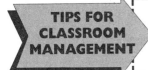

TIPS FOR CLASSROOM MANAGEMENT

IF children need additional support, **THEN** complete Working with "Lionel in the Winter" on page T375 in the *Full Sails* Teacher's Edition.

COMPREHENSION CHECK

All Levels These questions can serve as models to meet the needs of the various language levels of your children.

PRE/EARLY PRODUCTION Are Lionel and Jeffrey playing in the snow? (yes)

EARLY PRODUCTION What do Lionel and Jeffrey make? (snowmen) Does the snowman face the street or the house? (the house)

SPEECH EMERGENCE Why does Lionel have the snowman face the house? (Possible responses: There is a lot for the snowman to see in the house; the snowman can guard the house.) Why do Lionel and Jeffrey go inside? (Possible responses: to get warm; to dry off; to get some hot cocoa)

INTERMEDIATE FLUENCY How did Lionel and Jeffrey build the snowman? Tell about it in order. (They rolled balls of snow. They put on a potato for a nose, marbles for eyes, and branches for arms. They gave the snowman a hat and a scarf.)

WRITE THE STEPS

All Levels Invite small groups of children to work together to write the steps for making a snowman. Suggest they brainstorm four or more steps. Have them write the steps and number them. Then encourage children to illustrate the steps with drawings. LISTENING/SPEAKING/WRITING

A TALKING SNOWMAN

Speech Emergence/Intermediate Fluency

Ask children to think about what the snowman in the story might say to Lionel and Jeffrey if he could talk. Invite them to think about what Lionel and Jeffrey would say in return. Then have children act out the conversation. LISTENING/SPEAKING

LANGUAGE EXPERIENCE

Speech Emergence/Intermediate Fluency

Invite children to think about what else Lionel and Jeffrey could do on a snowy day. Suggest that they write a story about one of those activities. Children can write the story using illustrations or they can dictate the story to you. Encourage all children to illustrate their writing. Have volunteers read their stories aloud. LISTENING/READING/WRITING

TRADE BOOK

What Can a Hippopotamus Be? by Mike Thaler. Parents' Magazine Press, 1975. A hippopotamus learns what jobs he cannot do when he experiments with what he might be when he grows up.

SCHOOL ↔ HOME CONNECTION

Have children read their snow stories to their family members. Children can share what their family members liked best about the snow stories.

Harcourt Brace School Publishers

Introducing the Literature

BUILDING BACKGROUND

Prior Knowledge

Talk with children about how people feel when friends move away from each other. Ask if children have ever left any friends behind. Invite volunteers to tell how they felt.

TPR: Total Physical Response

To develop the concept of communicating with friends who move away, remind children that friends often take trips, talk on the telephone, or write letters to each other. Demonstrate each form of communication. Ask children to join you in pretending they are taking a boat trip to visit an old friend who lives far away. Then name the other forms of communication, and have children respond by acting out each one.

Develop Oral Language

Display the following rhyme, and read it aloud, emphasizing the beat. Then invite children to clap to the beat as they join you in repeating the rhyme several times. You may want to point to the following illustrations in "Jenny's Journey": boat, sail, sea, waves, dolphins, seagulls, ocean.

> I'll sail my boat over the sea,
> Over the sea so blue.
> I'll sail my boat over the waves,
> To see a friend so true.
>
> Dolphins jump and seagulls fly,
> Over the ocean so wide.
> I'll sail my boat over the sea,
> To be at my best friend's side!

BUILDING CONCEPTS

Use Poster 24: "Visit a Friend"

Poster 24 shows a way to visit friends who have moved far away. Point to the girl in the boat, and ask how she will visit her friend. Ask what she must travel over to visit her friend. (sea, ocean, waves) Continue to use Poster 24 to talk about ways people stay in touch with friends who move far away.

Write these concept words from "Jenny's Journey" on the board: *boat, sail, sea, ocean, dolphin, seagulls, waves.* Draw pictures of unfamiliar words.

Rereading

Invite children to reread the rhyme with you. Have volunteers pantomime the actions.

MEETING INDIVIDUAL NEEDS

Speech Emergence Ask children to name other forms of transportation that they might use if they were taking a trip to visit a friend.

Copying Master

Use page 95 to help make the concepts more comprehensible.

TIPS FOR CLASSROOM MANAGEMENT

You may want to have children read a translation of "Jenny's Journey" in their first language with family members. See *Anthology Translation Booklets.*

Jenny's Journey

A. Pretend you are on this boat. Trace the line from Start to End. Tell a friend what you see. Use the words in the waves.

boat   sail   sea   ocean   dolphin   seagulls   waves

Start

End

B. Take this page home. Tell your family about your trip on the boat.

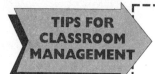

To prepare children to read "Jenny's Journey," use page 96 to provide additional concepts and language.

BEFORE READING PAGES 184–193

Invite children to look through the illustrations on pages 184–193. Hold up pages 186–187, and say

- This is Jenny. She is reading a letter.
- The letter is from Maria.
- They are best friends.
- Maria has moved away.
- Maria is lonely. Jenny writes to Maria.
- Jenny says she will sail on a boat to see Maria.

As you hold up pages 188–191 for all to see, point to the appropriate pictures, and say

- Jenny writes about a pretend trip she takes to see Maria.
- Jenny sails by other boats.
- Jenny sails past the Statue of Liberty.
- Jenny sails under a bridge.
- She falls asleep. She wakes up all alone.

Hold up pages 192–193, and say

- Jenny feels lonely.
- Dolphins jump out of the water.
- Seagulls land on the boat.
- Jenny feeds the animals.
- Jenny remembers feeding animals at the zoo with Maria.

Pantomime the actions of the animals. Then ask children these questions:

PREPRODUCTION/EARLY PRODUCTION

- Is Jenny sailing on a boat? (yes)
- Who is Jenny pretending to visit, a friend or a sister? (friend)

SPEECH EMERGENCE/INTERMEDIATE FLUENCY

- What does Jenny see on her trip? (Possible responses: boats, Statue of Liberty, bridge)

BEFORE READING PAGES 194–202

Encourage children to look at the illustrations on pages 194–202. Then hold up pages 194–195 for all to see, and say

- A big boat passes Jenny.
- Someone asks where Jenny is going.
- Jenny says she is going to visit Maria.

As you hold up pages 196–199 for all to see, point to the appropriate pictures, and say

- Jenny sails past islands.
- She gets caught in a storm.
- The wind is strong. The waves are high.
- Then the storm stops.
- Jenny takes out her guitar.
- She sings about Maria and her trip.

Pantomime Jenny strumming her guitar and singing. Then hold up pages 200–201, and say

- Jenny sees land. Maria is waiting.
- The friends are happy to see each other.

Hold up page 202, and say

- Jenny tells Maria that she will really come to see her someday.
- Jenny ends her letter.

Then ask children these questions:

PREPRODUCTION/EARLY PRODUCTION

- Does Jenny play a guitar? (yes)
- Does Jenny really go to see Maria? (no)

SPEECH EMERGENCE/INTERMEDIATE FLUENCY

- What does Jenny do after the storm? (Possible responses: She plays her guitar; she goes to see Maria.)
- What does Jenny say to Maria at the end of her letter? (Jenny tells Maria that she will really come to see her someday.)

Harcourt Brace School Publishers

READING THE LITERATURE Have children join the Strategic Reading group and read the selection with English-fluent partners.

Responding to the Literature

TIPS FOR CLASSROOM MANAGEMENT

IF children need additional support, **THEN** complete Working with "Jenny's Journey" on page T431 in the *Full Sails* Teacher's Edition.

COMPREHENSION CHECK

All Levels These questions can serve as models to meet the needs of the various language levels of your children.

PREPRODUCTION Do Jenny and Maria really get to see each other in this story? (no)

EARLY PRODUCTION Do Jenny and Maria write letters or call on the telephone? (write letters)

SPEECH EMERGENCE What does Jenny tell the person on the big boat? (She is going to visit Maria.) What does Jenny sing about when she plays the guitar? (Possible responses: the trip, Maria)

INTERMEDIATE FLUENCY Do you think Jenny and Maria will ever get to really see each other? (Possible response: Yes, they seem to be good friends and they will see each other someday.)

LIST TEN ITEMS

All Levels Invite children to think about what they would take with them if they were going on a boat trip across the sea. Then have children work in small groups to make a list of ten items. Children can write the list, dictate the list to you, or draw pictures of the items. Ask each group to share their list. LISTENING/SPEAKING/WRITING

> What We Would Take on a Boat Trip
> 1. food   2. book
> 3. water   4. guitar
> 5. flashlight   6. radio
> 7. clothes   8. toothbrush
> 9. life jacket   10. comb

NAMING SEA ANIMALS

Early Production/Speech Emergence Point out to children that dolphins are animals that live in the sea. Brainstorm with children names of other sea animals, such as tuna and sea star. List the names of the animals on the board, and encourage children to name the animals in their first language. LISTENING/SPEAKING

LANGUAGE EXPERIENCE

Speech Emergence/Intermediate Fluency Invite children to write a story about a child who takes a trip to visit a friend. As volunteers dictate sentences, write them on chart paper. Make a copy for each child. Encourage children to illustrate the story. LISTENING/SPEAKING/WRITING

ESL/TITLE I LIBRARY

Nine Men Chase a Hen by Barbara Gregorich. School Zone, 1992. This counting rhyme tells of a humorous rivalry between hens and a group of men. **Available on ESL/Title I Audiocassette.**

SCHOOL ↔ HOME CONNECTION
Encourage children to read their illustrated stories to their family members. Invite them to report back on how their family members liked the stories.

Dreams

BUILDING BACKGROUND

Prior Knowledge

Discuss bedtime with children. Ask volunteers what they do at night before they go to sleep. Encourage them to describe what their rooms look like. Do they ever see any shadows on the walls? If so, encourage children to describe them. Ask them if they dream, and invite volunteers to tell about dreams they have had.

TPR: Total Physical Response

To further develop the concept of shadows, shine a bright light on a classroom wall and make a shadow with your body. Demonstrate how the shadow changes size as you move closer to or farther away from the wall. Use your hands to make shadow shapes for children. Then have them follow directions and make their own shadow shapes.

Develop Oral Language

Display the following rhyme and read it aloud, emphasizing the rhyming words. Then invite children to reread the rhyme with you several times. You may want to point to the following in "Dreams": bed, covers, shadow.

> It's dark outside, and I'm in bed.
>   But I'm not asleep tonight.
> I just can't seem to sleep or dream.
>   I pull the covers tight.
>
> Then I sit up and look around.
>   A shape is on the wall!
> The shape gets bigger as I move.
>   Why, it's my shadow — that's all!

BUILDING CONCEPTS

Use Poster 25: "Dreaming"

Poster 25 shows a dream scene. Ask volunteers to tell where the boy is. Have children describe what the boy is doing. (Possible response: He is dreaming about a mouse chasing a dog.) Ask children to point to a shadow. Have them find the paper mouse in the room. Encourage them to describe the paper mouse's shadow. Use Poster 25 to help children express ideas about sleep, dreams, and shadows.

Write these concept words from "Dreams" on the board: *bed, dream, asleep, shadow, bigger.* Read them aloud as you point to each one. Use each word in a sentence that helps clarify its meaning.

Rereading

Invite children to read the rhyme with you and to point to any illustrations of concept words they see on Poster 25.

MEETING INDIVIDUAL NEEDS

Intermediate Fluency Invite children to describe a funny dream that they had recently.

Copying Master

Use page 99 to help make the concepts more comprehensible.

TIPS FOR CLASSROOM MANAGEMENT

You may want to have children read a translation of "Dreams" in their first language with family members. See *Anthology Translation Booklets.*

Harcourt Brace School Publishers

Dreams

A. Work with a partner. Talk about the picture. Read and answer the questions. Use the pictures and words to help you.

❶ Is the boy in bed or in school?

_____

- - - - - - - - - - - - - - - - - - - -

_____

bed   school

❷ Is the boy awake or asleep?

_____

- - - - - - - - - - - - - - - - - - - -

_____

awake   asleep

❸ Does the boy dream or play?

_____

- - - - - - - - - - - - - - - - - - - -

_____

dream   play

❹ Do the animals have shadows or hats?

_____

- - - - - - - - - - - - - - - - - - - -

_____

shadows   hats

B. Share this page with your family.

Harcourt Brace School Publishers

To prepare children to read "Dreams," use page 100 to provide additional concepts and language.

BEFORE READING PAGES 14–21

Read aloud the title, and look at the illustrations on pages 14–21 with children. Then hold up pages 14–15 for all to see, and say

- This is Roberto. This is Amy.
- They are friends.
- Roberto made a paper mouse in school.
- He shows the mouse to Amy.
- Amy asks if the mouse does anything.
- Roberto says he doesn't know.
- Roberto puts the mouse on the windowsill.

Hold up pages 16–19 for all to see, point to the appropriate pictures, and say

- Now it is bedtime.
- Everybody says good-night.
- Everybody starts dreaming.
- Roberto doesn't dream.
- He can't fall asleep.

Hold up pages 20–21 for all to see, and say

- Roberto looks out the window.
- He sees his friend's cat.
- A dog is chasing the cat.
- The cat is trapped in a box.
- Roberto thinks about what to do.

Then ask children these questions:

PREPRODUCTION/EARLY PRODUCTION

- Does Roberto talk to his friend Amy? (yes)
- Does Roberto show Amy a paper mouse or a paper bird? (paper mouse)

SPEECH EMERGENCE/INTERMEDIATE FLUENCY

- Who can't fall asleep in this story? (Roberto)
- What does Roberto see when he looks out his window? (Possible response: Roberto sees his friend's cat. A dog is chasing the cat. The cat gets trapped.)

BEFORE READING PAGES 22–29

Look at the illustrations on pages 22–29 with children. Then hold up pages 22–25 for all to see, point to the appropriate pictures, and say

- The paper mouse falls off the windowsill.
- It falls down.
- It makes a shadow on the wall.
- The shadow gets bigger and bigger.
- The shadow scares the dog.
- The dog runs away.
- The cat runs home.
- Roberto is proud of his mouse.
- Roberto goes back to bed.

Hold up pages 26–29 for all to see, and say

- Now it is morning.
- Everybody is getting up.
- Roberto does not get up.
- Roberto is asleep.
- Roberto is dreaming!

Then ask children these questions:

PREPRODUCTION/EARLY PRODUCTION

- Does a book fall off the windowsill? (no)
- Does the mouse make a shadow on the wall? (yes)
- Does the shadow get bigger or smaller? (bigger)

SPEECH EMERGENCE/INTERMEDIATE FLUENCY

- What does the shadow scare? (the dog)
- Where does the cat go? (home)
- What happens the next morning? (Possible response: Everybody gets up. Roberto is asleep. He is dreaming.)
- Why do you think Roberto is sleeping and dreaming instead of getting up? (Possible response: He stayed awake late last night. He is tired.)

READING THE LITERATURE   Have children join the Strategic Reading group and read the selection with English-fluent partners.

Harcourt Brace School Publishers

Responding to the Literature

TIPS FOR CLASSROOM MANAGEMENT

IF children need additional support, **THEN** complete the Working with "Dreams" activity found on page T45 in the *All Smiles* Teacher's Edition.

COMPREHENSION CHECK

All Levels These questions can serve as models to meet the needs of the various language levels of your children.

PRE/EARLY PRODUCTION Does Roberto leave the paper mouse on the windowsill? (yes)

SPEECH EMERGENCE Who chases the cat into the box? (a dog) What scares away the dog? (the shadow made by Roberto's mouse)

INTERMEDIATE FLUENCY Could this story take place in real life? Why or why not? (Possible response: Yes, everything in this story could happen to real people and to real animals.) If the mouse had not fallen off the windowsill, what do you think Roberto could have done to help the cat? (Possible response: He could have asked his mother to help.)

SHADOW SHAPES

All Levels Invite small groups to look for shadows in a brightly lit classroom or outside on the school grounds. Then have group members work together to describe the different kinds of shadows they see and to name the objects that make those shadows.
LISTENING/SPEAKING/WRITING

Shadow Shape	What Made It
tall, long	tree trunk
big, square	school building
short, round	wastepaper basket

I CAN'T SLEEP!

Early Production/Speech Emergence Ask children to pretend that they are home in their rooms. Have them imagine that it is nighttime and they can't sleep. Then invite volunteers to act out what they might do in their rooms until they can fall asleep. You can spark ideas by suggesting that children pretend they are reading, looking out the window, or watching shadows on the wall.
LISTENING/SPEAKING

WRITING STORIES

Speech Emergence/Intermediate Fluency
Encourage children to write their own funny stories about shadows at night. Have children illustrate what happens at the beginning, in the middle, and at the end of their stories. Children can then show their pictures and read aloud the stories they wrote.
LISTENING/SPEAKING/READING/WRITING

TRADE BOOK
Jafta by Hugh Lewin. Carolrhoda, 1981. A boy named Jafta compares himself with the animals of his native land.

SCHOOL ↔ HOME CONNECTION
Invite children to take home their stories and share them with their families. Have them ask family members about funny experiences they have had with shadows.

Introducing the Literature

BUILDING BACKGROUND

Prior Knowledge

Begin a discussion about dogs. Have volunteers describe dogs they have seen. Encourage them to name the different parts of a dog, such as the head, legs, body, and tail. Then invite children to say the word *dog* in their first language.

TPR: Total Physical Response

To develop this concept further, display several pictures of dogs and then invite children to imitate your actions as you pretend to be a dog. As you perform, tell children what you are doing, such as *sit up, wag your tail, bark, run to the window, give your paw.*

Develop Oral Language

Display the following rhyme and read it aloud, emphasizing the beat. Then have children reread the rhyme with you several times. You may want to use pictures of a dog to help children visualize the words *head, neck, back, chest, legs, stomach,* and *tail.*

> Each time I try to wash my pet,
> I end up getting soaking wet!
> I wash his head; his neck gets rubbed.
> Then his back and chest get scrubbed.
>
> I wash his legs and stomach clean.
> He'll be the prettiest dog you've seen!
> From head to tail, he's as wet as can be —
> And then he shakes it off on ME!

BUILDING CONCEPTS

Use Poster 26: "All About Dogs"

Poster 26 shows the parts of a dog and some things a boy and his dog can do together. Ask a volunteer to name the pet shown on the poster. Ask children to point to the dog's head, back, neck, chest, stomach, legs, and tail as you read the labels. Then invite volunteers to tell what a person can do with a pet dog.

Write these concept words from "Henry and Mudge in the Green Time" on the board: *tail, neck, back, chest, stomach, legs.* Have children point to the appropriate body part on Poster 26 as you say each concept word.

Rereading

Invite children to read the rhyme with you again. Have them point to any illustrated concept words they see on Poster 26.

Speech Emergence Ask children to talk about the parts of a dog that are on a dog's head, such as the eyes, nose, and ears, and what these parts do.

Copying Master

Use page 103 to help make the concepts more comprehensible.

TIPS FOR CLASSROOM MANAGEMENT

You may want to have children read a translation of "Henry and Mudge in the Green Time" in their first language with family members. See *Anthology Translation Booklets.*

Harcourt Brace School Publishers

AME _____

Henry and Mudge in the Green Time

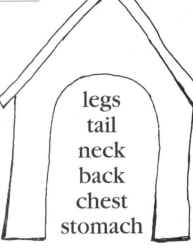

legs
tail
neck
back
chest
stomach

A. Talk about the words in the doghouse with a partner. What part do people not have? Write that word next to its picture. Then write the other words.

B. Share this page with your family.

To prepare children to read "Henry and Mudge in the Green Time," use page 104 to provide additional concepts and language.

BEFORE READING PAGES 34–40

Read aloud the title of the story. You may wish to explain that "the green time" is the season of spring. Then look at the illustrations on pages 34–40 with children. Hold up pages 35–38 for all to see, point to the appropriate pictures, and say

- This is Henry.
- This is Henry's dog, Mudge.
- Henry is going to give Mudge a bath.
- Mudge does not like baths.
- Henry looks for the dog shampoo.
- Henry hooks up the water hose.
- Mudge tries to hide.
- Mudge goes under the steps.
- Mudge is too big!
- Henry finds Mudge.

Hold up pages 39–40 for all to see, and say

- Henry takes Mudge to the front yard.
- Henry gets Mudge wet.
- Mudge hates it.
- Mudge looks like a big walrus.

If possible, display a picture of a walrus. Then ask children these questions:

PREPRODUCTION/EARLY PRODUCTION

- Is this story about a boy and his dog? (yes)
- Does the boy give his dog a bath or a bone? (a bath)
- Does the dog like the bath? (no)

SPEECH EMERGENCE/INTERMEDIATE FLUENCY

- What is the name of Henry's dog? (Mudge)
- Why does Mudge try to hide under the stairs? (He does not like baths.)
- What does Mudge look like when he gets wet? (a big walrus)

BEFORE READING PAGES 41–47

Look at the illustrations on pages 41–47 with children. Then hold up pages 41–43 for all to see, point to the appropriate pictures, and say

- Henry washes Mudge with shampoo.
- Henry scrubs Mudge's head.
- He scrubs Mudge's neck and back.
- He scrubs Mudge's chest and stomach.
- He scrubs Mudge's legs and tail.
- Mudge hates to be scrubbed.
- Then Henry hoses Mudge down again.
- Now it's time for Mudge to get Henry!

Hold up pages 44–47 for all to see, point to the appropriate pictures, and say

- Mudge starts shaking.
- He shakes his head.
- He shakes his neck and back.
- He shakes his chest and stomach.
- He shakes his legs and tail.
- Mudge is almost dry.
- Henry is very wet!
- Mudge wags his tail.
- Henry dries himself with a towel.
- Henry and Mudge are both happy.

Then ask children these questions:

PREPRODUCTION/EARLY PRODUCTION

- Does Henry get wet when he gives Mudge a bath? (yes)
- Who shakes off the water after the bath, Henry or Mudge? (Mudge)

SPEECH EMERGENCE/INTERMEDIATE FLUENCY

- What parts of Mudge get scrubbed? (head, neck, back, chest, stomach, legs, tail)
- How does Mudge get dry? (He shakes.)
- How does Henry get dry? (with a towel)

READING THE LITERATURE Have children join the Strategic Reading group and read the selection with English-fluent partners.

Harcourt Brace School Publishers

Responding to the Literature

TIPS FOR CLASSROOM MANAGEMENT

IF children need additional support, **THEN** complete Working with "Henry and Mudge in the Green Time" on page T89 in the *All Smiles* Teacher's Edition.

COMPREHENSION CHECK

All Levels These questions can serve as models to meet the needs of the various language levels of your children.

PREPRODUCTION Is Mudge a dog? (yes) Is Henry a boy? (yes)

EARLY PRODUCTION Does Mudge get washed or does Henry get washed? (Mudge)

SPEECH EMERGENCE Who is supposed to get wet when Henry gives Mudge a bath? (Mudge) Who gets wet when Henry gives Mudge a bath? (both Henry and Mudge)

INTERMEDIATE FLUENCY Why does Henry like to give Mudge a bath on a hot day? (Possible response: Henry can play with the water and cool off.) Why do you think Mudge does not like getting a bath? (Possible responses: He does not like getting wet; he does not like to be scrubbed.)

IF MUDGE COULD TALK

All Levels Have children work in groups. Ask them to pretend that Mudge can talk. Have children in each group think about what Mudge might say to Henry while he is having his bath. Invite children to write Mudge's words on paper. Then ask the groups to share their ideas. LISTENING/SPEAKING/WRITING

HENRY AND MUDGE

Early Production/Speech Emergence Invite children to work with a partner. Ask the partners to look through the pictures in "Henry and Mudge in the Green Time" and choose a part of the story to act out. Then provide time for children to practice their scene together. Invite children to act out their scene for their classmates. LISTENING/SPEAKING

WRITING ABOUT A PET

Speech Emergence/Intermediate Fluency
Ask children to write their own stories about giving a bath to a pet. They might want to write about a cat or a horse. Encourage them to illustrate their stories. Then ask children to share their drawings and read their stories aloud. LISTENING/READING/WRITING

TRADE BOOK
Spots, Feathers, and Curly Tails by Nancy Tafuri. Greenwillow, 1988. Readers are given picture clues and asked to identify animals.

SCHOOL ↔ HOME CONNECTION
Encourage children to take home their stories and read them to family members. Ask them to report back on what their families thought about the stories.

Introducing the Literature

Pets

BUILDING BACKGROUND

Prior Knowledge

Talk with children about pets they have or would like to have. Ask volunteers to describe their pets and to tell their pets' names. Invite them to tell how they play with their pets, and what they do to help care for their pets. Encourage children to give the animal name of their pets in their first language.

TPR: Total Physical Response

To develop this concept further, pantomime a dog chasing after a ball. Talk with children about what you are doing. Then invite children to follow you as you give directions and pantomime other pets in action, such as a cat pouncing on a stuffed mouse, a rabbit hiding from a dog, or a bird flying. Have children take turns pantomiming different animals for you and other classmates to guess.

Develop Oral Language

Display and read aloud the following rhyme. Then invite children to join in as you repeat the rhyme several times. You can point to pictures in "Pets" to help children visualize the pets named in the rhyme and some of the action words, such as *chase* and *pounce*.

Visit a pet store and you will see
How very busy pets can be.
You might see a bird crack a nut,
Or a hamster hide in a little grass hut.
Some kittens pounce on a rubber ball,
And puppies chase each other through the hall.
Guinea pigs exercise on a wheel,
While snakes hunt mice—what a meal!
Visit a pet store and you will see
How very busy pets can be!

BUILDING CONCEPTS

Use Poster 27: "Pets in Action"

Poster 27 shows pets in action. Ask volunteers to name the pet shown in each row. (dog, cat, guinea pig) Ask children to tell ways the dogs in the pictures get exercise. (by chasing a ball, by going for a walk) Repeat by asking similar questions about the pets in the other two rows. Then use Poster 27 to help children talk more about pets.

Write these concept words from "Pets" on the board. Read each word aloud as you point to it: *pets, chase, crack, pounce, hunt, exercise, hide.* Use pantomime to help children understand the meanings of the words.

Rereading

Invite children to reread the rhyme with you. Encourage them to clap each time they hear a pet name or a pet action.

Early Production Ask children to draw a picture of a pet in action. Encourage children to dictate a caption for their picture.

Copying Master

Use page 107 to help make the concepts more comprehensible.

TIPS FOR CLASSROOM MANAGEMENT

You may want to have children read a translation of "Pets" in their first language with family members. See *Anthology Translation Booklets.*

Harcourt Brace School Publishers

Pets

A. Talk with a partner about the pictures and words in the bone.
Write a word that tells about each picture.

pets   hunt   chase   pounce   crack   hide

_____

- - - - - - - - - - - - - - - - -

_____

_____

- - - - - - - - - - - - - - - - -

_____

_____

- - - - - - - - - - - - - - - - -

_____

B. Share this page with your family.

TIPS FOR CLASSROOM MANAGEMENT

To prepare children to read "Pets," use page 108 to provide additional concepts and language.

BEFORE READING PAGES 54–61

Read aloud the title of the book. Then look through the illustrations on pages 54–61 with children. Display pages 54–55, and say

- This is a rabbit. This is a parakeet.
- This is a puppy. A puppy is a baby dog.
- This is a fish. This is a kitten.
- A kitten is a baby cat.
- All these animals are pets.

Display pages 56–57, and say

- These are puppies. Puppies are dogs.
- Dogs need to go outside for walks.
- Dogs like to chase balls and sticks.
- Dogs bark when they are excited.

Act out barking. Then display pages 58–59, and say

- This is a parakeet. It is a pet bird.
- A parakeet lives in a cage.
- A parakeet uses its beak to crack open seeds.
- A parakeet has claws.

Display pages 60–61, and say

- This is a kitten.
- This is a cat. Cats have soft fur.
- Cats like to be petted.
- Cats play and hunt at night.

Act out purring. Then ask children these questions:

PREPRODUCTION/EARLY PRODUCTION

- Is this story about wild animals? (no)
- Is this story about pets? (yes)

SPEECH EMERGENCE/INTERMEDIATE FLUENCY

- How do dogs get exercise? (They go outside for walks. They chase balls and sticks.)
- How would you describe a parakeet? (It is a bird. It has feathers, a sharp beak, and claws.)

BEFORE READING PAGES 62–68

Look through pages 62–68 with children. Then display pages 62–63, and say

- This is a guinea pig.
- Guinea pigs get fat if they don't exercise.
- Guinea pigs are shy.
- They hide in the woodchips.

Then display pages 64–65, and say

- This is a rabbit.
- Rabbits hear very well.
- Rabbits can run fast.
- Rabbits eat carrots and fresh greens.
- Rabbits dig holes with their front paws.

Pantomime a rabbit nibbling on a carrot. Then display pages 66–68, and say

- This is a goldfish.
- Goldfish live in water.
- They have tails and fins.
- They have gills and scales.
- Goldfish use their tails and fins to swim.
- Goldfish must be fed every day.
- This is a hamster.
- Hamsters like to eat seeds.
- They have sharp front teeth.

Pantomime feeding goldfish. Then ask children these questions:

PREPRODUCTION/EARLY PRODUCTION

- Do guinea pigs like to hide? (yes)
- Do goldfish live in water or in cages? (water)

SPEECH EMERGENCE/INTERMEDIATE FLUENCY

- Why do guinea pigs need to exercise? (They like food. They eat too much and get fat.)
- How are goldfish different from the other pets in this story? (They live in water.)

READING THE LITERATURE Have children join the Strategic Reading group and read the selection with English-fluent partners.

Harcourt Brace School Publishers

Responding to the Literature

TIPS FOR CLASSROOM MANAGEMENT

IF children need additional support, **THEN** complete Working with "Pets" on page T131 in the *All Smiles* Teacher's Edition.

COMPREHENSION CHECK

All Levels These questions can serve as models to meet the needs of the various language levels of your children.

PREPRODUCTION Is the story about farm animals? (no) Is the story about house pets? (yes)

EARLY PRODUCTION Do pets need to sit around, or do they need exercise? (exercise)

SPEECH EMERGENCE What are some ways pets communicate with you? (dogs wag their tails, birds chirp, cats purr)

INTERMEDIATE FLUENCY What did you learn about the pets in the story? (Responses will vary.) Which pet would you like to have? Why? (Responses will vary.)

PET POSTERS

All Levels Invite groups of children to select one pet from the story and make a "What We Know" poster about that pet. Encourage them to include information from the story as well as their own knowledge about the pet. Groups can then share their posters with each other. LISTENING/SPEAKING/WRITING

WANTED: A CLASSROOM PET

Early Production/Speech Emergence Invite small groups to decide what animal would make a good classroom pet. Ask them to write a list called "How to Care for the Pet." Encourage them to draw a picture of the pet and to display their lists under the pet's picture. Encourage children to tell why the animal they selected would make a good classroom pet. LISTENING/SPEAKING/WRITING

WRITING A STORY

Speech Emergence/Intermediate Fluency Invite children to write their own story entitled "Pets." Students can write summaries about the pets in the selection, or they can write about other pets. Ask them to draw pictures of the pets and what the pets are doing. Help children staple their pages together to make a book. Invite them to read their stories aloud. LISTENING/SPEAKING/READING/WRITING

TRADE BOOK

Mary Had a Little Lamb by Sarah Joseph Hale. Scholastic, 1990. The nursery rhyme is brought up-to-date with contemporary photos.

SCHOOL ↔ HOME CONNECTION

Invite children to share their story with family members. Encourage them to ask family members what pets they have had or would like to have.

Introducing the Literature

The Adventures of Snail at School

BUILDING BACKGROUND

Prior Knowledge

Talk with children about being a new student at school. You may want to have volunteers tell how they felt when they first came to your school. Discuss what it was like getting to know new children and a new teacher. Discuss what it was like learning one's way around a new building.

TPR: Total Physical Response

To develop the concept of school and the locations within a school, have children brainstorm a list of places they go while in school, such as the cafeteria, media center, or computer lab. List each one on the board. Then, as you point to each one, demonstrate what children do at each location. For example, as you point to the media center, you might act out reading a book. Finally, have children act out what they do at each of the places you point out and name.

Develop Oral Language

Display the following rhyme, and read it aloud. Have children reread the rhyme with you several times. You may want to point to the following in "The Adventures of Snail at School: The New Student": school, office, hallway, seat, classroom, students, class.

> Sometimes it's hard to be new at school.
> You have to act brave and pretend to be cool.
> The principal in the office looks sort of mean,
> And each hallway is long and crowded in
>   between.
> When you look for a seat in a classroom that's
>   new,
> All the other students have their eyes upon you.
> Then one student in class smiles and looks glad.
> Maybe a new school isn't so bad!

BUILDING CONCEPTS

 Use Poster 28: "A New School"
Poster 28 shows a school. Point to a classroom and an office. Ask children who will sit in the seats in the classroom. (students) Tell children the office they see is the principal's office. Ask children to talk about what is going on in the hallway. Point out the fire extinguisher in the hallway. Explain to children what it is and how it is used. Use Poster 28 to help children increase their understanding of a school setting.

Write these concept words on the board: *school, student, class, office, hallway, classroom, seat*. Use each one in a sentence to clarify its meaning.

Rereading

Invite children to read the rhyme with you again. Have them point to any illustrated concept words they see on Poster 28.

 Intermediate Fluency Invite partners to brainstorm reasons why going to school is important.

Copying Master

Use page 111 to help make the concepts more comprehensible.

TIPS FOR CLASSROOM MANAGEMENT

You may want to have children read a translation of "The Adventures of Snail at School: The New Student" in their first language with family members. See *Anthology Translation Booklets.*

Harcourt Brace School Publishers

The Adventures of Snail at School: The New Student

A. Work with a partner. Read the picture names. Tell where you would find each person or thing. Use the other words to help you.

classroom

school   flower

_____

- - - - - - - - - - - -

_____

student

sun   class

_____

- - - - - - - - - - - -

_____

seat

lamp   classroom

_____

- - - - - - - - - - - -

_____

principal

office   ocean

_____

- - - - - - - - - - - -

_____

fire extinguisher

seat   hallway

_____

- - - - - - - - - - - -

_____

B. Share this page with your family.

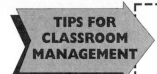

To prepare children to read "The Adventures of Snail at School: The New Student," use page 112 to provide additional concepts and language.

BEFORE READING PAGES 76–83

Read aloud the title of the story. Look at the illustrations on pages 76–83 with children. Then hold up pages 76–79 for all to see, and say

- This is Mrs. Harvey. She is a teacher.
- A new student is coming to school.
- The new student is in the principal's office.
- Mrs. Harvey wants someone to get the new student.
- This is Snail.
- Snail says he will get the new student.

Then hold up pages 80–83 for all to see, and say

- Snail goes down the hallway.
- Snail gets to the principal's office.
- Snail sees a fire extinguisher.
- The fire extinguisher is by the door.
- Snail says he will put it back.
- Snail pushes the fire extinguisher.
- He hears a noise. Hisssss!
- He grabs the fire extinguisher.
- It blasts off. Snail is on it!
- Snail goes into space.

Then ask children these questions:

PREPRODUCTION/EARLY PRODUCTION

- Does Snail go to the principal's office or to the library? (the principal's office)
- Does Snail see a fire or a fire extinguisher? (a fire extinguisher)

SPEECH EMERGENCE/INTERMEDIATE FLUENCY

- Where is the new student? (in the office)
- What does Snail see in front of the office door? (a fire extinguisher)
- What happens when Snail pushes the fire extinguisher? (The fire extinguisher blasts off. Snail goes into space.)

BEFORE READING PAGES 84–92

Look at the illustrations on pages 84–92 with children. Then hold up pages 84–88, point to the appropriate pictures, and say

- Snail lands on another planet.
- Snail thinks he sees monsters.
- Snail looks closer.
- They are not monsters.
- They look like Snail. This is Edie.
- She welcomes Snail to the planet.
- Snail goes to a party on the planet.
- He sees a big cake.
- Snail must go back to his classroom.
- Snail and Edie take off for Earth.
- They go in a rocket.

Hold up pages 89–92 for all to see, and say

- Snail and Edie land at Snail's school.
- Snail tells Mrs. Harvey what happened.
- Mrs. Harvey thinks Snail is making up a story.
- Mrs. Harvey thinks Edie is the new student.
- Snail says Edie comes from another planet.
- Mrs. Harvey does not believe Snail.
- Then Mrs. Harvey sees Edie floating.
- Mrs. Harvey is confused.
- She decides not to ask Snail anything.

Then ask children these questions:

PREPRODUCTION/EARLY PRODUCTION

- Does Snail land on another planet? (yes)
- Do the people on the planet look like monsters or like Snail? (Snail)

SPEECH EMERGENCE/INTERMEDIATE FLUENCY

- How does Snail get back to his school? (Edie takes him in a rocket.)
- How does Mrs. Harvey feel at the end of the story? (She is confused.)

READING THE LITERATURE Have children join the Strategic Reading group and read the selection with English-fluent partners.

Harcourt Brace School Publishers

Responding to the Literature

TIPS FOR CLASSROOM MANAGEMENT

IF children need additional support, **THEN** complete the Intervention Strategies found on page T193 in the *All Smiles* Teacher's Edition.

COMPREHENSION CHECK

All Levels These questions can serve as models to meet the needs of the various language levels of the children.

PREPRODUCTION Is Snail a teacher? (no) Is Snail a student? (yes)

EARLY PRODUCTION Is Mrs. Harvey the teacher or the principal? (the teacher) Is there a new student or a new teacher in the principal's office? (a new student)

SPEECH EMERGENCE Who goes to get the new student? (Snail) Where does Snail find the fire extinguisher? (in the hallway; near the office)

INTERMEDIATE FLUENCY What happens to Snail when he blasts off on the fire extinguisher? (He lands on another planet. He meets Edie. Edie takes him back to Earth in a rocket.)

WELCOME TO OUR SCHOOL

All Levels Invite children to work in small groups. Ask them to brainstorm a list of things they could do to make a new student feel comfortable in school. Encourage them to record their ideas on paper. Invite a member of each group to read the ideas aloud and to discuss them with the other members of the group. LISTENING/SPEAKING/READING/WRITING

> Welcome to Our School
> Be friendly.
> Show the new student around the school.
> Invite the new student to play.

GIVING DIRECTIONS

Early Production/Speech Emergence Remind children that Snail went from his classroom to the principal's office to get the new student. Then ask children to pretend they are giving directions to a new student. Have them work together to tell how they would get from their own classroom to the principal's office. LISTENING/SPEAKING

WRITING A STORY

Speech Emergence/Intermediate Fluency Ask children to imagine that Snail returns to Edie's planet to be a new student at her school. Invite them to write a story about what happens to Snail. Encourage children to illustrate their stories with drawings. Invite them to read their stories aloud. READING/WRITING

ESL/TITLE I LIBRARY

Hurray for Snail! by John Stadler. HarperCollins, 1984. Snail gets a big hit. **Available on ESL/Title I Audiocassette.**

SCHOOL ↔ HOME CONNECTION
Have children take home their stories and share them with their family members. Encourage them to ask family members if they have ever been a new student at school.

Harcourt Brace School Publishers

Introducing the Literature

Planets

BUILDING BACKGROUND

Prior Knowledge

Begin a discussion about space. Encourage volunteers to name things in space, such as stars, planets, the sun, and the moon. Talk about how people travel in space. Invite volunteers to share the names in their first language of space-related objects such as the sun, stars, or the moon.

TPR: Total Physical Response

To develop this concept further, invite children to join you on a pretend shuttle flight into space. Lead them to "put" on space suits and a space helmet. Then ask them to sit in their seats for "blast off." Count backward from ten to one for the blast off. When the shuttle reaches outer space, have children follow you as you model the actions and give directions. You might begin by saying, *Look to your left and point to the moon. Cover your eyes—we're getting close to the sun.*

Develop Oral Language

Display the following rhyme and read it aloud. Have children reread the rhyme with you several times. You may want to point to the following photographs in "Planets": planets, space, world, moons, rings, Earth.

> Nine round planets move in space,
> Circling around the sun.
> Nine round planets move in space,
> And our green world is one.
>
> Some of the planets have moons and rings.
> One looks like a star.
> Nine round planets move in space,
> And Earth is where we are.

BUILDING CONCEPTS

Use Poster 29: "The Solar System"

Poster 29 shows our solar system. Read aloud the names of the planets. Have children point to the planet that is our world. Have volunteers tell what is in the middle of the solar system. (the sun) Ask which planet is closest to the sun and which is farthest away. (Mercury; Pluto) Then invite children to point to the planets on Poster 29 that have rings.

Write these concept words from "Planets" on the board: *planets, world, star, moons, rings.* Read each one aloud. Use pictures to illustrate the meanings of unfamiliar words.

Rereading

Invite children to read the rhyme with you again. Have them point to any illustrated concept words they see on Poster 29.

MEETING INDIVIDUAL NEEDS

Preproduction Display a globe. Invite children to spin the globe. Tell children that this is our planet, Earth.

Copying Master

Use page 115 to help make the concepts more comprehensible.

TIPS FOR CLASSROOM MANAGEMENT

You may want to have children read a translation of "Planets" in their first language with family members. See *Anthology Translation Booklets.*

Harcourt Brace School Publishers

Planets

A. Work with a partner. Think of a word to finish each sentence. Use the words in the box to help you.

planets	world	star	moons	rings

Our sun is a

_____

- - - - - - - - - - - - - - - - - - - -

_____

These are

_____

- - - - - - - - - - - - - - - - - - - -

_____ .

This planet has

_____

- - - - - - - - - - - - - - - - - - - -

_____ .

This planet has two

_____

- - - - - - - - - - - - - - - - - - - -

_____ .

The planet Earth is our

_____

- - - - - - - - - - - - - - - - - - - -

_____ .

B. Share this page with your family.

Harcourt Brace School Publishers

BEFORE READING PAGES 106–117

Share the title of the story and look at the illustrations on pages 106–117 with children. Then hold up pages 108–109 for all to see, and say

- This is our world.
- Our world is a planet.
- Our world is named Earth.

Hold up pages 110–113 for all to see, and say

- There are nine planets.
- The planets move around the sun.
- Our sun is a star.
- Planets close to the sun are hot.
- Planets far from the sun are cold.

Hold up pages 114–115 for all to see, and say

- This is Mercury. Mercury is a planet.
- Mercury is the closest planet to the sun.
- This is Venus. Venus is a planet.
- We can see Venus from Earth.
- It looks like a star.

Hold up pages 116–117 for all to see, and say

- This is Mars. Mars is a planet.
- Mars is red. It has two moons.
- This is Jupiter. Jupiter is a planet.
- Jupiter is very big.
- It is the biggest planet.

Then ask children these questions:

PREPRODUCTION/EARLY PRODUCTION

- Is this story about stars? (no)
- Is this story about planets? (yes)

SPEECH EMERGENCE/INTERMEDIATE FLUENCY

- Which planet is very hot? (Mercury)
- What is special about the planet Mars? (It is red. It has two moons.)

BEFORE READING PAGES 118–122

Look at the illustrations on pages 118–122 with children. Then hold up pages 118–119 for all to see, and say

- This is Saturn. Saturn is a planet.
- Saturn has rings.
- The rings are made of ice and rock.
- This is Uranus. Uranus is a planet.
- Uranus has rings, too.
- Uranus has lots of moons.

Hold up pages 120–121, and say

- This is Neptune.
- Neptune is a planet.
- Neptune is far from Earth.
- It is almost too far for us to see.
- This is Pluto. Pluto is a planet.
- Pluto is very far from the sun.
- Pluto is very cold.

Hold up page 122 for all to see, and say

- Earth is our planet.
- Earth is just right for people.
- Someday people might visit other planets.

Then ask children these questions:

PREPRODUCTION/EARLY PRODUCTION

- Is Saturn a planet? (yes)
- Is Uranus a star? (no)
- Are Neptune and Pluto close to Earth or far from Earth? (far)

SPEECH EMERGENCE/INTERMEDIATE FLUENCY

- Which planet is just right for people? (Earth)
- Why do you think Pluto is very cold? (It is very far from the sun.)
- Which planet would you like to visit? Why? (Responses will vary.)

Harcourt Brace School Publishers

READING THE LITERATURE Have children join the Strategic Reading group and read the selection with English-fluent partners.

Responding to the Literature

TIPS FOR CLASSROOM MANAGEMENT

IF children need additional support, **THEN** complete Working with "Planets" on page T255 in the *All Smiles* Teacher's Edition.

COMPREHENSION CHECK

All Levels These questions can serve as models to meet the needs of the various language levels of your children.

PREPRODUCTION Do some planets have rings? (yes) Do some planets have moons? (yes)

EARLY PRODUCTION Is Earth a planet or a moon? (a planet) What planet do we live on? (Earth)

SPEECH EMERGENCE Which planet is closest to the sun? (Mercury) Which planet is farthest from the sun? (Pluto)

INTERMEDIATE FLUENCY Why do you think Earth is just right for people? (Possible responses: Earth has water and air; Earth is not too hot or too cold.) Why do you think people want to visit other planets? (Responses will vary.)

PACK FOR SPACE

All Levels Form groups that include children at all levels of English proficiency. Invite volunteers to brainstorm lists of things that they would take with them if they were going on a long journey into space. Help children record their lists on chart paper. Then invite the groups to share their ideas with each other. LISTENING/SPEAKING/WRITING

Things to Take on a Trip into Space

space suit	food and water
picture of family	fresh air
map of space	space boots
camera	books to read

SPACE RIDDLES

Early Production/Speech Emergence Pose the following or similar riddles about space and invite volunteers to answer them. Then encourage children to make up riddles of their own to ask each other. LISTENING/SPEAKING

- This is bright. It twinkles. (star)
- This is a planet. We live on it. (Earth)
- This is bright. We see it at night. (moon)

WRITING ABOUT A TRIP

Speech Emergence/Intermediate Fluency Invite partners to choose the planet that they would most like to visit. Ask them to write a story about a trip to that planet. Have them describe what the planet looks like and what they would do there. Encourage children to use the information in "Planets" to help them write their stories. Children can illustrate their stories with pictures. WRITING

TRADE BOOK

I Want to Be an Astronaut by Byron Barton. HarperCollins, 1988. A child describes this wish.

SCHOOL ↔ HOME CONNECTION

Invite children to take home their stories and read them to their family members. Have them ask family members which planet they would most like to visit, and why.

Harcourt Brace School Publishers

Introducing the Literature

Geraldine's Baby Brother

BUILDING BACKGROUND

Prior Knowledge
Talk with children about families. Ask them to name some family members, such as mother and father. Help them recognize that families also include relatives such as aunts, uncles, cousins, and grandparents. Invite children to say in their first language the names of family members.

TPR: Total Physical Response
Demonstrate for children the following finger play. Then have children do the finger play as you model the actions and say the rhyme aloud.

> Here are Mama's knives and forks. *(Interlock fingers, palms up.)* This is Papa's table. *(Keep fingers interlocked and turn palms down.)* This is sister's looking glass. *(Make peak of two forefingers.)* And this is baby's cradle. *(Add peak of little fingers.)*

Develop Oral Language
Display and read aloud the following rhyme, emphasizing the rhyming words. Then ask children to reread the rhyme with you several times. You can use illustrations in "Geraldine's Baby Brother" to help children understand that *brother, uncle, mama, aunt,* and *papa* are names of family members.

> Mama and Papa and I
> Made a very nice group of three.
> When Uncle and Aunt came to visit,
> We made a big family.
>
> Now I have a new baby brother.
> All he does is eat, sleep, and shout.
> Everyone runs to take care of him,
> And I don't like being left out!

BUILDING CONCEPTS

Use Poster 30: "A Family"
Poster 30 displays an extended family. Point to the children in the poster, and explain that the baby is a boy. Ask volunteers whether the baby is the girl's brother or sister. (brother) Then point to other family members. Help children recognize that they are the mama, papa, brother, uncle, and aunt.

Write these concept words from "Geraldine's Baby Brother" on the board: *brother, uncle, mama, aunt, papa*. Use each one in a sentence to clarify its meaning.

Rereading
Invite children to read the rhyme with you again. Have them use some of the concept words in sentences about their family members.

MEETING INDIVIDUAL NEEDS

Challenge Ask children to tell how a cousin is related to them.

Copying Master
Use page 119 to help make the concepts more comprehensible.

TIPS FOR CLASSROOM MANAGEMENT

You may want to have children read a translation of "Geraldine's Baby Brother" in their first language with family members. See *Anthology Translation Booklets.*

Harcourt Brace School Publishers

Geraldine's Baby Brother

A. Look at the pictures. Read with a partner. Write a word to answer each riddle.

brother   uncle   mama   aunt   papa

❶ You are my child.
I am a woman.
Who am I?

_____

❷ You are my child.
I am a man.
Who am I?

_____

❸ I am your mother's brother.
I am a man.
Who am I?

_____

❹ I am your mother's sister.
I am a woman.
Who am I?

_____

❺ We have the same mother.
I am a boy.
Who am I?

_____

B. Share this page with your family.

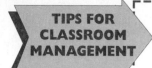

To prepare children to read "Geraldine's Baby Brother," use page 120 to provide additional concepts and language.

BEFORE READING PAGES 134–141

Look at the illustrations on pages 134–141 with children. Hold up pages 135–138 for all to see, point to the appropriate pictures, and say

- This is Geraldine.
- This is Geraldine's baby brother, Willie.
- Willie cries a lot.
- This is Uncle Albert.
- Geraldine is wearing earmuffs.
- She doesn't want to hear Willie.
- The doorbell rings. Willie starts to cry.
- Mama comes out of the kitchen.
- Aunt Bessie comes downstairs.
- Papa gets up from the sofa.
- Mrs. Wilson is at the door.
- She has presents for Willie and Geraldine.
- Geraldine hides behind the chair.

Hold up pages 139–141 for all to see, point to the appropriate pictures, and say

- Willie cries all morning.
- Aunt Bessie picks him up.
- Papa carries Willie around the house.
- Uncle Albert makes funny faces for Willie.
- Willie is still crying at lunchtime.
- Mama wonders where Geraldine is.

Then ask children these questions:

PREPRODUCTION/EARLY PRODUCTION

- Is Willie a baby? (yes)
- Does Geraldine like Willie? (no)

SPEECH EMERGENCE/INTERMEDIATE FLUENCY

- Who are the people in Geraldine's family? (Brother Willie, Mama, Papa, Uncle Albert, Aunt Bessie)
- What does Geraldine do so she can't hear Willie crying? (She wears earmuffs.)

BEFORE READING PAGES 142–148

Look at the illustrations on pages 142–148 with children. Then hold up pages 142–144 for all to see, point to the appropriate pictures, and say

- Geraldine is in her room.
- Geraldine doesn't want to talk to Mama.
- Later, Geraldine goes into the kitchen.
- She says she is going to go to bed.
- Willie is still crying.
- Papa waits for Geraldine by the bathroom.
- Aunt Bessie made a special dinner for her.
- Geraldine says she is not hungry.

Hold up pages 145–148, point to the appropriate pictures, and say

- Geraldine hears Willie at night.
- She goes to Willie's room.
- She tells Willie to stop crying.
- Willie makes funny faces.
- Geraldine reads stories to Willie.
- Mama finds Geraldine and Willie in the morning. They are both asleep.
- Geraldine wants to give Willie his bottle.
- Mama wants to hug Geraldine.

Then ask children these questions:

PREPRODUCTION/EARLY PRODUCTION

- Does Geraldine go to Willie's room at night? (yes)
- Who finds Geraldine and Willie asleep, Mama or Papa? (Mama)

SPEECH EMERGENCE/INTERMEDIATE FLUENCY

- What does Geraldine do in Willie's room? (She reads stories to Willie.)
- How do you think Geraldine feels about her baby brother at the end of the story? (Possible response: She likes him.)

READING THE LITERATURE Have children join the Strategic Reading group and read the selection with English-fluent partners.

Harcourt Brace School Publishers

Responding to the Literature

TIPS FOR CLASSROOM MANAGEMENT

IF children need additional support, **THEN** complete Working with "Geraldine's Baby Brother" on page T321 in the *All Smiles* Teacher's Edition.

COMPREHENSION CHECK

All Levels These questions can serve as models to meet the needs of the various language levels of your children.

PREPRODUCTION Is this story about Geraldine and a friend? (no)

EARLY PRODUCTION At the beginning of the story, was Geraldine happy or unhappy to have a baby brother? (unhappy)

SPEECH EMERGENCE What did Geraldine's baby brother do most of the time? (cry)

INTERMEDIATE FLUENCY Why do you think people pay a lot of attention to babies? (Possible responses: Babies cry a lot; babies cannot do things for themselves; they need much care and attention.)

CREATE LISTS

All Levels Form groups that include children at various levels of English proficiency. Invite children to brainstorm things that are nice about having a new baby in the family. Then have them brainstorm things that are not so nice. Ask children to make a list of their ideas on paper. LISTENING/SPEAKING/WRITING

| A New Baby in the Family ||
Nice	Not So Nice
People come to visit.	The baby gets all
The baby makes	the attention.
funny noises.	The baby cries a lot.
The baby is cute.	The baby can't play.
We are older than	Mom and Dad are very
the baby.	busy.

IN OTHER WORDS

Early Production/Speech Emergence Point out that Geraldine calls her parents *Mama* and *Papa*. Then invite children to give other names that Geraldine could use, such as *mother, father, mom, dad, mommy,* and *daddy*—or other names children use at home. List responses on the board. Children may enjoy sharing stories about how some family names came to be. LISTENING/SPEAKING

WRITING STORIES

Speech Emergence/Intermediate Fluency Ask children to think about what Geraldine might do to help care for her baby brother. Then invite them to write stories about something that Geraldine does to help care for her brother, Willie. Children can illustrate their stories. Ask volunteers to share their stories. LISTENING/READING/WRITING

ESL/TITLE I LIBRARY

Just Like Daddy by Frank Asch. Aladdin, 1981. A young bear tells how he does his daily activities just like his daddy. **Available on ESL/Title I Audiocassette.**

SCHOOL ↔ HOME CONNECTION

Have children take home their stories and share them with their family members. Encourage them to ask family members about what they were like when they were babies.

Introducing the Literature

BUILDING BACKGROUND

Prior Knowledge

Talk with children about their favorite foods. Encourage volunteers to tell how their favorite food is made and what ingredients go into it. Ask them to tell what they like to drink with their favorite food. Encourage children to name some foods and beverages that are popular in their native countries.

TPR: Total Physical Response

Have children follow you as you model the actions and give the following directions.

> Do you like tacos with lots of cheese?
> Well, stand up and clap if you please.
> Do you like peanut butter and jelly?
> Then, stand up tall and rub your belly.
> Do you like eating cookies in bed?
> Please sit in your seat and pat your head.

Develop Oral Language

Display the following rhyme, and read it aloud in a humorous tone of voice. Then have children reread the rhyme with you several times. You may want to point to the following illustrations in "Julius": ice cubes, coffee, bed, jar, peanut butter.

> I like ice cubes in my coffee.
> I like cereal in my tea.
> I like cookies in my bed,
> But the crumbs bother me.
>
> I can eat a jar of peanut butter.
> I like pickles with ice cream.
> But why is it when I eat these foods,
> I always have a strange dream?

BUILDING CONCEPTS

Use Poster 31: "Our Favorite Foods"

Poster 31 shows some popular foods. Have children point to the jar of peanut butter. Ask what they think the girl is eating. Ask what the father is eating and drinking. Have children point to the crumbs on the plate of cookies. Ask what is in the glass. Use Poster 31 to help children express their understanding of foods. Children can also name the other foods pictured around the border of the poster.

Write these concept words from "Julius" on the board: *ice cubes, coffee, peanut butter, cookies, crumbs, jar.* Use each one in a sentence to clarify its meaning.

Rereading

Invite children to read the rhyme with you again. Have them point to pictures that illustrate the concept words on Poster 31.

MEETING INDIVIDUAL NEEDS

Speech Emergence Help children to name two things to eat and two things to drink.

Copying Master

Use page 123 to help make the concepts more comprehensible.

TIPS FOR CLASSROOM MANAGEMENT

You may want to have children read a translation of "Julius" in their first language with family members. See *Anthology Translation Booklets.*

Harcourt Brace School Publishers

Julius

coffee
cookies
crumbs
ice cubes
jar
peanut butter

A. Talk and write about each picture.

_____

- - - - - - - - - - - - - - - - -

_____

- - - - - - - - - - - - - - - - -

_____

- - - - - - - - - - - - - - - - -

_____

- - - - - - - - - - - - - - - - -

B. Talk with a partner. Which foods or drinks do you like?

C. Share this page with your family.

TIPS FOR CLASSROOM MANAGEMENT To prepare children to read "Julius," use page 124 to provide additional concepts and language.

BEFORE READING PAGES 154–163

Share the title, and look at the illustrations on pages 154–163 with children. Then hold up pages 156–159, point to the appropriate pictures, and say

- This is Maya.
- This is Maya's granddaddy.
- Granddaddy brings Maya a present.
- The present is something that will teach Maya to share.
- The present is a big pig named Julius.
- Maya's parents do not think they will like Julius.
- Maya loves Julius.

Hold up pages 160–163, point to the appropriate pictures, and say

- Julius eats a lot of food.
- He drinks coffee and eats peanut butter.
- He rolls in flour when he wants Maya to bake cookies.
- Julius makes messes.
- He leaves crumbs on the sheets.
- He never picks up his towels.
- He stays up late watching old movies.
- He plays records when everybody is reading.

Then ask children these questions:

PREPRODUCTION/EARLY PRODUCTION

- Does Maya's granddaddy bring her a pig as a present? (yes)
- Is the pig neat or messy? (messy)

SPEECH EMERGENCE/INTERMEDIATE FLUENCY

- What is the name of Maya's pig? (Julius)
- What does Julius like to eat and drink? (coffee, peanut butter, cookies)

BEFORE READING PAGES 164–173

Look at the illustrations on pages 164–173 with children. Then hold up pages 164–168, point to the appropriate pictures, and say

- Maya knows other things about Julius.
- Julius is fun to take on walks.
- Julius likes to try on funny clothes in stores.
- Julius tries on hats with Maya.
- Julius plays on the swings with Maya.
- Julius protects Maya from scary things.

Hold up pages 169–173, point to the appropriate pictures, and say

- Maya loves Julius.
- Julius teaches Maya how to dance.
- Julius loves Maya.
- Maya teaches Julius how to stay clean.
- Maya teaches Julius how to act nice.
- Maya shares what she learned from Julius.
- Maya shows her friends how to swing.
- Maya shows her friends how to try on hats and dance.
- Julius shares what he learned from Maya.
- Julius acts nice around Maya's parents.
- Julius likes living with Maya.

Then ask children these questions:

PREPRODUCTION/EARLY PRODUCTION

- Is Julius afraid of scary things? (no)
- Does Julius show Maya how to dance or how to sing? (dance)

SPEECH EMERGENCE/INTERMEDIATE FLUENCY

- What are some things that Maya and Julius like to do together? (Possible responses: They go for walks; they try on clothes; they play on the swings; they dance; they eat peanut butter from a jar.)

READING THE LITERATURE Have children join the Strategic Reading group and read the selection with English-fluent partners.

Harcourt Brace School Publishers

Responding to the Literature

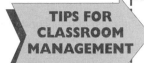

TIPS FOR CLASSROOM MANAGEMENT

IF children need additional support, **THEN** complete the Working with "Julius" activity found on page T367 in the *All Smiles* Teacher's Edition.

COMPREHENSION CHECK

All Levels These questions can serve as models to meet the needs of the various language levels of your children.

PREPRODUCTION Is Julius a dog? (no)
EARLY PRODUCTION Who gives Maya the pig, her parents or her granddaddy? (granddaddy)
SPEECH EMERGENCE Before Maya gets Julius as a present, what does she want? (a horse or an older brother) Where did Julius come from? (Alaska)
INTERMEDIATE FLUENCY Would you like to have a pig as a pet? Why or why not? (Responses will vary.) How does sharing things make everyone in the story happy? (Possible responses: Julius and Maya learn new things; Maya's parents like Julius because of what he learns from Maya.)

FOODS THAT GO TOGETHER

All Levels Point out to children that some foods seem to go together, such as cookies and milk or bread and butter. Have children work in groups to make a list of foods that go together. Some children might like to cut and paste magazine pictures to illustrate food combinations. Invite groups to share their ideas. LISTENING/SPEAKING/WRITING

Foods That Go Together
cookies and milk
bread and butter
taco chips and salsa
cereal and bananas

ACT IT OUT

Preproduction/Early Production Using commands such as the following, invite children to act out the way they would eat each food:

Sip hot soup.
Crunch on a taco chip.
Drink a glass of cold orange juice.
Eat a sticky peanut butter sandwich.

Then have children take turns naming other foods. Invite classmates to act out how they would eat the foods named. LISTENING/SPEAKING

WRITING STORIES

Speech Emergence/Intermediate Fluency
Ask children to imagine that Maya's father took Julius shopping for clothes. Invite them to write funny stories about what happened in the store. Children can draw pictures and then write about the events. WRITING

TRADE BOOK
Mrs. Sato's Hens by Laura Min. Good Year Books, 1994. A young girl and an elderly woman count the eggs in the nest every day of the week.

SCHOOL ↔ HOME CONNECTION
Invite children to take home their stories and read them to their family members. Have them report back how their family members liked the stories.

Harcourt Brace School Publishers

Introducing the Literature

New Shoes for Silvia

BUILDING BACKGROUND

Prior Knowledge
Discuss clothing with children. Encourage volunteers to name things they wear on their feet and things they wear on their bodies. Then talk with them about what they do with shoes and clothes that are too big or too small for them. As articles of clothing are discussed, children can share the names for these items in their first languages.

TPR: Total Physical Response
To further develop the concept of clothes we wear, bring in several articles of different sizes of clothing. Name each one, and invite children to try them on. Give directions, such as *Try on the red skirt* or *Put on the pair of pants.* If possible, bring in several different pairs of shoes. As a child is trying on an article of clothing, other children can predict whether or not it will fit by holding up a sign saying *Too Big, Too Small,* or *Just Right.*

Develop Oral Language
Display the following rhyme, and read it aloud. Then have volunteers reread the rhyme with you several times.

My new shoes are big,
And they don't fit my feet.
My old shoes are small,
And the buckles don't meet.

My skirt is the wrong size,
As anyone can see.
It's hard to wear clothes that fit
When you're growing like me!

BUILDING CONCEPTS

Use Poster 32: "Clothing"
Poster 32 shows articles of clothing.
Point to the articles of clothing, and read the labels with children. Then have children point to the shoes. Ask children if they know their shoe size. Have them point to an article of clothing that they would wear and name it for them. Use Poster 32 to help children understand articles of clothing.

Write these concept words from "New Shoes for Silvia" on the board: *shoes, buckles, wear, fit, size, skirt.* Bring in a skirt and shoes with buckles to help children understand these concept words.

Rereading
Invite children to read the rhyme with you again. As you read, have them point to any illustrations of concept words they see on Poster 32.

Preproduction Provide children with magazines that have lots of pictures. Name an article of clothing, and ask children to find a picture of that item in the magazines.

Copying Master
Use page 127 to help make the concepts more comprehensible.

TIPS FOR CLASSROOM MANAGEMENT

You may want to have children read a translation of "New Shoes for Silvia" in their first language with family members. See *Anthology Translation Booklets.*

Harcourt Brace School Publishers

New Shoes for Silvia

buckles

shoes

skirt

A. Talk about the pictures with a partner. Write about each picture.

_____

- - - - - - - - - - - - - -

_____

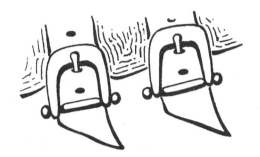

_____

- - - - - - - - - - - - - -

_____

_____

- - - - - - - - - - - - - -

_____

B. Work with a partner. Read the questions. Answer each question.

❶ Do you plant shoes or wear shoes? Why?

❷ Do shoes come in sizes or in jars? Why?

❸ Should shoes fit or fly?

C. Share this page with your family.

TIPS FOR CLASSROOM MANAGEMENT To prepare children to read "New Shoes for Silvia," use page 128 to provide additional concepts and language.

BEFORE READING PAGES 182–193

Read aloud the title, and look at the illustrations on pages 182–193 with children. Then hold up pages 184–189, point to the pictures, and say

- This is Silvia. This is Silvia's family.
- One day, a package arrives from Tía Rosita.
- Silvia gets a new pair of shoes.
- The shoes are red with buckles.
- Silvia loves the shoes.
- But the shoes are too big.
- Her mom tells her to put them away.

Hold up pages 190–193, point to pictures, and say

- Silvia tries the shoes on again in the morning. They are still too big.
- Silvia uses the shoes as beds for her dolls.
- Silvia tries the shoes on again a week later.
- The shoes are still too big.
- Silvia uses the shoes to make a train.
- Silvia tries the shoes on again a week later.
- The shoes are still too big.
- She ties string to the shoes and pulls them.

Then ask children these questions:

PREPRODUCTION/EARLY PRODUCTION

- Is this story about Silvia? (yes)
- What gift did Silvia get? (shoes)

SPEECH EMERGENCE/INTERMEDIATE FLUENCY

- Why can't Silvia wear her new shoes? (The shoes are too big.)
- What does Silvia do with the shoes instead of wearing them? (She makes beds for her dolls. She uses the shoes as a train. She ties string to the shoes and pulls them.)

BEFORE READING PAGES 194–203

Look at the illustrations on pages 194–203 with children. Then hold up pages 194–199, and say

- Another week passes.
- Silvia's shoes are still too big.
- She fills them with shells and pebbles.
- Many weeks pass.
- Silvia plays with friends and helps her mother.
- Silvia forgets to try on her new shoes.
- One day Silvia's mother writes a letter.
- The letter is to Tía Rosita.
- Silvia thinks about the shoes again.
- She dusts off the shoes with her skirt.
- She tries on the shoes. They fit!

Hold up pages 200–203, and say

- Silvia goes to the post office.
- She wears her new shoes.
- The red shoes are just the right size now!
- Silvia is happy.

Then ask children these questions:

PREPRODUCTION/EARLY PRODUCTION

- Do the shoes ever fit Silvia? (yes)
- Is Silvia happy when the shoes fit? (yes)
- Does Silvia forget about the shoes for a while or try them on every day? (forgets about them)

SPEECH EMERGENCE/INTERMEDIATE FLUENCY

- What happens that reminds Silvia about the red shoes? (Silvia's mother writes a letter to Tía Rosita.)
- Why do Silvia's shoes fit her at the end of the story? (Silvia has grown.)
- Have you ever had new shoes that were too big? What did you do with them? (Responses will vary.)

Harcourt Brace School Publishers

READING THE LITERATURE Have children join the Strategic Reading group and read the selection with English-fluent partners.

Responding to the Literature

TIPS FOR CLASSROOM MANAGEMENT

IF children need additional support, **THEN** complete the Intervention Strategies found on page T423 in the *All Smiles* Teacher's Edition.

COMPREHENSION CHECK

All Levels These questions can serve as models to meet the needs of the various language levels of the children.

PREPRODUCTION Does this story take place in another country? (yes)

EARLY PRODUCTION Does Silvia get a new skirt or new shoes? (new shoes)

SPEECH EMERGENCE How do members of Silvia's family describe the color of the shoes? (red as the setting sun; red as the color of a rose; red as the inside of a watermelon)

INTERMEDIATE FLUENCY How do you know that Silvia likes the new shoes? (She is sad when she can't wear them. She keeps trying them on.) Why do you think Silvia's mother doesn't want Silvia to wear the shoes when she first gets them? (Responses will vary.)

ON YOUR FEET

All Levels Place children in small groups. Invite children to brainstorm names of different kinds of footwear. Have them list the footwear on chart paper and draw an illustration of each type. Post children's work on a wall in the classroom, and encourage groups to compare what they wrote.
LISTENING/SPEAKING/READING/WRITING

sneakers

sandals

boots
clogs

FUN WITH SHOES

Preproduction/Early Production Remind children that when Silvia could not wear her new shoes, she used her shoes for different things. Invite children to draw a picture showing something else Silvia might have done with her shoes before they fit her. Have children display and discuss their pictures. LISTENING/SPEAKING

WRITING STORIES

Speech Emergence/Intermediate Fluency
Invite children to think about what might have happened if Tía Rosita had sent Silvia a new skirt. Help them write stories that include a beginning, a middle, and an ending. Encourage children to illustrate their work and share their stories. LISTENING/READING/WRITING

ESL/TITLE I LIBRARY
Eat Your Peas, Louise! by Pegeen Snow. Childrens Press, 1985. The only thing that will make Louise eat her peas is the word *please*.
Available on ESL/Title I Audiocassette.

SCHOOL ↔ HOME CONNECTION
Have children take home their stories and read them to their family members. Invite them to talk to their family members about the kinds of shoes they like to wear.